Angels Watching Over Me

By Gigi Rogers

CONTENTS

DEDICATION

To my best friend and confidant Jesus who walked with me through this journey and to my husband who has always encouraged me to do *whatever I want to do,*

ACKNOWLEDGMENTS

To my family and friends who have tirelessly encouraged me to write this book. I will forever be grateful.

To my editor and creative partners Pat and Christina who helped me.

To my kids who gave me their love and encouragement to finish the book

Thank you and love you all.

"GiGi"

ONE

What is an Angel?

The word *"angel"* actually comes from the Greek word *aggelos*, which means *"messenger."* The matching Hebrew word *mal'ak* has the same meaning.

We know God created the angels:

> *Psalm 148:2-5 (NKJV)*
> *² Praise Him, all His angels; Praise Him, all His hosts!*
> *³ Praise Him, sun and moon; Praise Him, all you stars of light! ⁴ Praise Him, you heavens of heavens, and you waters above the heavens! ⁵ Let them praise the name of the Lord, For He commanded and they were created.*

> *Colossians 1:16 (NKJV)*
> *¹⁶ For by Him all things were created that are in heaven and that are on earth, visible and invisible, whether thrones or dominions or principalities or powers. All things were created through Him and for Him.*

What do we know about Angels?

They were originally created holy:

> *Luke 9:26 (NKJV)*
> *²⁶ For whoever is ashamed of Me and My words, of him the Son of Man will be ashamed when He comes*

in His own glory, and in His Father's and of the holy angels.

They are more powerful than humans:

> *Psalm 103:20-21 (NKJV)*
> *[20] Bless the Lord, you His angels, who excel in strength, who do His word. Heeding the voice of His word. [21] Bless the Lord, all you His hosts, You ministers of His, who do His pleasure.*

> *2 Peter 2:11 (NKJV)*
> *[11] whereas angels, who are greater in power and might, do not bring a reviling accusation against them before the Lord.*

They are not omniscient (knowing everything):

> *Matthew 24:36 (NKJV)*
> *[36] "But of that day and hour no one knows, not even the angels of heaven, but My Father only.*

They are not omnipotent (having unlimited power, able to do anything):

> *Romans 8:38-39 (NKJV)*
> *[38] For I am persuaded that neither death nor life, nor angels nor principalities nor powers, nor things present nor things to come, [39] nor height nor depth, nor any other created thing, shall be able to separate us from the love of God which is in Christ Jesus our Lord.*
> *Jude 1:9 (NKJV)*
> *[9] yet Michael the archangel in contending with the devil, when he disputed about the body of Moses, dared to bring against him a reviling accusation but*

said, "The Lord rebuke you!"

They are not omnipresent (all present):

Daniel 10:13 (NKJV)
13 But the prince of the kingdom of Persia withstood me twenty-one days; and behold, Michael, one of the chief princes, came to help me, for I had been left alone there with the kings of Persia.

They are often described as the "host of heaven" and are innumerable:

Luke 2:13 (NKJV)
13 And suddenly there was with the angel a multitude of the heavenly host praising God and saying: 14 "Glory to God in the highest, And on earth peace, goodwill toward men!"

Hebrews 12:22 (NKJV)
22 But you have come to Mount Zion and to the city of the living God, the heavenly Jerusalem, to an innumerable company of angels

Revelation 5:11 (NKJV)
11 Then I looked, and I heard the voice of many angels around the throne, the living creatures, and the elders; and the number of them was ten thousand times ten thousand, and thousands of thousands,

Angels are not subject to death:

Luke 20:34-36 (NKJV)
34 Jesus answered and said to them, "The sons of this age marry and are given in marriage. 35 But those

who are counted worthy to attain that age, and the resurrection from the dead, neither marry nor are given in marriage; ³⁶ *nor can they die anymore, for they are equal to the angels and are sons of God, being sons of the resurrection.*

Angels are spirit beings but can appear in human form humans:

Hebrews 1:14 (NKJV)
¹⁴ *Are they not all ministering spirits sent forth to minister for those who will inherit salvation?*

Genesis 18:1-19 (NKJV)
¹ *Then the Lord appeared to him by the terebinth trees of Mamre, as he was sitting in the tent door in the heat of the day.* ² *So he lifted his eyes and looked, and behold, three men were standing by him; and when he saw them, he ran from the tent door to meet them, and bowed himself to the ground,* ³ *and said, "My Lord, if I have now found favor in Your sight, do not pass on by Your servant.* ⁴ *Please let a little water be brought, and wash your feet, and rest yourselves under the tree.* ⁵ *And I will bring a morsel of bread, that you may refresh your hearts. After that you may pass by, inasmuch as you have come to your servant." They said, "Do as you have said."* ⁶ *So Abraham hurried into the tent to Sarah and said, "Quickly, make ready three measures of fine meal; knead it and make cakes."* ⁷ *And Abraham ran to the herd, took a tender and good calf, gave it to a young man, and he hastened to prepare it.* ⁸ *So he took butter and milk and the calf, which he had prepared, and set it before them; and he stood by*

them under the tree as they ate. ⁹Then they said to him, "Where is Sarah your wife?" So he said, "Here, in the tent." ¹⁰ And He said, "I will certainly return to you according to the time of life, and behold, Sarah your wife shall have a son." (Sarah was listening in the tent door, which was behind him.) ¹¹ Now Abraham and Sarah were old, well advanced in age; and Sarah had passed the age of childbearing. ¹² Therefore Sarah laughed within herself, saying, "After I have grown old, shall I have pleasure, my lord being old also?" ¹³ And the Lord said to Abraham, "Why did Sarah laugh, saying, 'Shall I surely bear a child, since I am old?' ¹⁴ Is anything too hard for the Lord? At the appointed time I will return to you, according to the time of life, and Sarah shall have a son."¹⁵ But Sarah denied it, saying, "I did not laugh," for she was afraid. And He said, "No, but you did laugh!" ¹⁶ Then the men rose from there and looked toward Sodom, and Abraham went with them to send them on the way. ¹⁷ And the Lord said, "Shall I hide from Abraham what I am doing, ¹⁸ since Abraham shall surely become a great and mighty nation, and all the nations of the earth shall be blessed in him? ¹⁹ For I have known him, in order that he may command his children and his household after him, that they keep the way of the Lord, to do righteousness and justice, that the Lord may bring to Abraham what He has spoken to him."

Genesis 19:1-3 (NKJV)
¹ Now the two angels came to Sodom in the evening, and Lot was sitting in the gate of Sodom. When Lot saw them, he rose to meet them, and he bowed himself with his face toward the ground. ² And he said, "Here now, my lords, please turn in to your servant's

house and spend the night, and wash your feet; then you may rise early and go on your way." And they said, "No, but we will spend the night in the open square." ³ But he insisted strongly; so they turned in to him and entered his house. Then he made them a feast, and baked unleavened bread, and they ate.

⁴ Now before they lay down, the men of the city, the men of Sodom, both old and young, all the people from every quarter, surrounded the house. ⁵ And they called to Lot and said to him, "Where are the men who came to you tonight? Bring them out to us that we may know them carnally."

Mark 16:5-10 (NKJV)
⁵ And entering the tomb, they saw a young man clothed in a long white robe sitting on the right side; and they were alarmed. ⁶ But he said to them, "Do not be alarmed. You seek Jesus of Nazareth, who was crucified. He is risen! He is not here. See the place where they laid Him. ⁷ But go, tell His disciples—and Peter—that He is going before you into Galilee; there you will see Him, as He said to you. ⁸ So they went out quickly and fled from the tomb, for they trembled and were amazed. And they said nothing to anyone, for they were afraid.

There are 2 categories of angels: unfallen and fallen. Unfallen or Holy angels are those who have remained holy throughout their existence.

Fallen angels by contrast, are those who have not maintained their holiness and have a special place reserved for them once this world ends.

There are the different types of angels? I have grouped

6

them into six categories:

1. <u>Archangels</u>: a chief angel, an order of angels

   1Thessalonia 4:16 (NKJV)
   ¹⁶ For the Lord Himself will descend from heaven with a shout, with the voice of an archangel, and with the trumpet of God. And the dead in Christ will rise first.

   Jude 1:9 (NKJV)
   ⁹ yet Michael the archangel in contending with the devil, when he disputed about the body of Moses, dared to bring against him a reviling accusation but said, "The Lord rebuke you!"

2. <u>Cherubim</u> are winged angelic beings described in biblical tradition as attending on God. Cherubim have four faces: one of a man, an ox, a lion, and an eagle. They have four conjoined wings covered with eyes, a lion's body figure, and they have ox's feet:

   Ezekiel 1:4-18 (NKJV)
   ⁴ Then I looked, and behold, a whirlwind was coming out of the north, a great cloud with raging fire engulfing itself; and brightness was all around it and radiating out of its midst like the color of amber, out of the midst of the fire. ⁵ Also from within it came the likeness of four living creatures. And this was their appearance: they had the likeness of a man. ⁶ Each one had four faces, and each one had four wings. ⁷ Their legs were straight, and the soles of their feet were like the soles of calves' feet. They sparkled like the color of burnished bronze. ⁸ The hands of a man were under their wings on their four sides; and each of the four had faces and wings. ⁹ Their wings

touched one another. The creatures did not turn when they went, but each one went straightforward. ¹⁰ As for the likeness of their faces, each had the face of a man; each of the four had the face of a lion on the right side, each of the four had the face of an ox on the left side, and each of the four had the face of an eagle. ¹¹ Thus were their faces. Their wings stretched upward; two wings of each one touched one another, and two covered their bodies. ¹² And each one went straightforward; they went wherever the spirit wanted to go, and they did not turn when they went. ¹³ As for the likeness of the living creatures, their appearance was like burning coals of fire, like the appearance of torches going back and forth among the living creatures. The fire was bright, and out of the fire went lightning. ¹⁴ And the living creatures ran back and forth, in appearance like a flash of lightning. ¹⁵ Now as I looked at the living creatures, behold, a wheel was on the earth beside each living creature with its four faces. ¹⁶ The appearance of the wheels and their workings was like the color of beryl, and all four had the same likeness. The appearance of their workings was, as it were, a wheel in the middle of a wheel. ¹⁷ When they moved, they went toward any one of four directions; they did not turn aside when they went. ¹⁸ As for their rims, they were so high they were awesome; and their rims were full of eyes, all around the four of them.

3. Elect Angels: The elect angels are those who stayed true to God during the original angelic rebellion:

   1 Timothy 5:21 (NKJV)

21 I charge you before God and the Lord Jesus Christ and the elect angels   that you observe these things without prejudice, doing nothing with partiality.

4. Guardian Angels are believed to be ministering angels sent forth to minister for those who will inherit salvation.

   Hebrews 1:14 (NASB)
   14 Are they not all ministering spirits, sent out to render service for the sake of those who will inherit salvation?

5. Seraphim are six winged beings around the throne of God. They fly and say "Holy, holy, holy Lord God almighty" Isaiah 6:1-3 Rev 4:8

   Isaiah 6:1-3 (NKJV)
   1 In the year that King Uzziah died, I saw the Lord sitting on a throne, high and lifted up, and the train of His robe filled the temple. 2 Above it stood seraphim; each one had six wings: with two he covered his face, with two he covered his feet, and with two he flew. 3 And one cried to another and said: "Holy, holy, holy is the Lord of hosts; the whole earth is full of His glory!"

   Revelation 4:1-8 (NKJV)
   1 After these things I looked, and behold, a door standing open in heaven. And the first voice, which I heard, was like a trumpet speaking with me, saying, "Come up here, and I will show you things which must take place after this." 2 Immediately I was in the Spirit; and behold, a throne set in heaven, and One sat on the throne. 3 And He who sat there was like a jasper and a sardius stone in appearance; and there was a

rainbow around the throne, in appearance like an emerald. ⁴ Around the throne were twenty-four thrones, and on the thrones I saw twenty-four elders sitting, clothed in white robes; and they had crowns of gold on their heads. ⁵ And from the throne preceded lightnings, thunderings, and voices. Seven lamps of fire were burning before the throne, which are the seven Spirits of God. ⁶ Before the throne there was a sea of glass, like crystal. And in the midst of the throne, and around the throne, were four living creatures full of eyes in front and in back. ⁷ The first living creature was like a lion, the second living creature like a calf, the third living creature had a face like a man, and the fourth living creature was like a flying eagle. ⁸ The four living creatures, each having six wings, were full of eyes around and within. And they do not rest day or night, saying: "Holy, holy, holy, Lord God Almighty, Who was and is and is to come!"

6. <u>Fallen</u> angels have fallen from their first estate. Led by Satan, who was originally a holy angel, the fallen angels defected, rebelled against God, and became sinful in their nature and work. Fallen angels are divided into two classes, free and bound.

But for the angels who fell:

Jude 1:6 (NKJV)
⁶ And the angels who did not keep their proper domain, but left their own abode, He has reserved in everlasting chains under darkness for the judgment of the great day

1 Corinthians 6:3 (NKJV)
³ Do you not know that we shall judge angels? How much more, things that pertain to this life?

Ephesians 6:12 (NKJV)
¹² For we do not wrestle against flesh and blood, but against principalities, against powers, against the rulers of the darkness of this age, against spiritual hosts of wickedness in the heavenly places.

Notice I did not include the death angel because this is not taught in the Bible as a group of angels specifically called to this task. The Bible says that angels do the work of God, which can include putting to death for example 185,000 Assyrians who had invaded Israel:

2 Kings 19:35 (NKJV)
³⁵ And it came to pass on a certain night that the angel of the Lord went out, and killed in the camp of the Assyrians one hundred and eighty-five thousand; and when people arose early in the morning, there were the corpses—all dead.

or the destruction of Sodom and Gomorrah;

Genesis 19:1-13 (NKJV)
¹ Now the two angels came to Sodom in the evening, and Lot was sitting in the gate of Sodom. When Lot saw them, he rose to meet them, and he bowed himself with his face toward the ground. ² And he said, "Here now, my lords, please turn in to your servant's house and spend the night, and wash your feet; then you may rise early and go on your way." And they said, "No, but we will spend the night in the open square." ³ But he insisted strongly; so they turned

in to him and entered his house. Then he made them a feast, and baked unleavened bread, and they ate.*4* Now, before they lay down, the men of the city, the men of Sodom, both old and young, all the people from every quarter, surrounded the house. *5* And they called to Lot and said to him, "Where are the men who came to you tonight? Bring them out to us that we may know them carnally." *6* So Lot went out to them through the doorway, shut the door behind him, *7* and said, "Please, my brethren, do not do so wickedly! *8* See now, I have two daughters who have not known a man; please, let me bring them out to you, and you may do to them as you wish; only do nothing to these men, since this is the reason they have come under the shadow of my roof." *9* And they said, "Stand back!" Then they said, "This one came in to stay here, and he keeps acting as a judge; now we will deal worse with you than with them." So they pressed hard against the man Lot, and came near to break down the door. *10* But the men reached out their hands and pulled Lot into the house with them, and shut the door. *11* And they struck the men who were at the doorway of the house with blindness, both small and great, so that they became weary trying to find the door. *12* Then the men said to Lot, "Have you anyone else here? Son-in-law, your sons, your daughters, and whomever you have in the city—take them out of this place! *13* For we will destroy this place, because the outcry against them has grown great before the face of the Lord, and the Lord has sent us to destroy it."

It is a common assumption that there was a death angel at the Passover but the Bible does not support that belief;

Exodus 12:12-13 (NKJV)

12 'For I will pass through the land of Egypt on that night, and will strike all the firstborn in the land of Egypt, both man and beast; and against all the gods of Egypt I will execute judgment: I am the Lord. 13 Now the blood shall be a sign for you on the houses where you are. And when I see the blood, I will pass over you; and the plague shall not be on you to destroy you when I strike the land of Egypt.

Did God do this by himself or did he give the order to one or maybe a group of Angels?   This will be one of those questions we ask God when we get to heaven

God alone is in charge of the time we die. No angel or demon can in any sense cause our death before the time God has willed it to occur.

TWO

My Belief

I believe God created all angels and heavenly beings. Why do I believe this? The most obvious reason, The Bible describes God as the Creator and Sustainer of Life.

John 1:1-3 – (NASB)
¹ In the beginning was the Word, and the Word was with God, and the Word was God. ² He was in the beginning with God. ³ All things came into being through Him, and apart from Him nothing came into being that has come into being.

Colossians 1:15-17 – (NASB)
¹⁵ He is the image of the invisible God, the firstborn of all creation. ¹⁶ For by Him all things were created, both in the heavens and on earth, visible and invisible, whether Thrones or dominions or rulers or authorities—all things have been created through Him and for Him. ¹⁷ He is before all things, and in Him all things hold together.

So if God made all things, especially powers and invisible things, wouldn't that include both angels and demons?

Wait a minute; did a Pastor's wife just tell you that God created demons? Well, not exactly. You see I believe that God created all angels and other heavenly beings, but something happened to those angelic beings after they left their first estate and now we have demonic beings that are talked about in Ephesians 6.

How can I believe that demons were once angels? We have to go back to the beginning. There was a heavenly being called Lucifer. Lucifer was a beautiful and magnificent being. He was referred to as the "Covering Cherubim." Just as the cherubim covered the mercy seat of the Ark of the Covenant, Lucifer was designed to be the Praise and Worship leader. There was nothing ordinary or plain about his appearance. The Bible says he was covered with some of the most beautiful and magnificent stones known to mankind. He had timbrels (tambourines) and pipes (wooden instrument with holes which makes different musical sounds) as part of his persona. I don't know if he carried them around with him, or if God made them into him.

> *Ezekiel 28:12-14 – (NASB)*
> *12 "Son of man, take up a lamentation over the king of Tyre and say to him, 'Thus says the Lord God, "You had the seal of perfection, Full of wisdom and perfect in beauty. 13 "You were in Eden, the garden of God; Every precious stone was your covering: The ruby, the topaz and the diamond; The beryl, the onyx and the jasper; The lapis lazuli, the turquoise and the emerald; And the gold, the workmanship of your settings and sockets, was in you on the day that you were created they were prepared. 14 "You were the anointed cherub who covers, and I placed you there. You were on the holy mountain of God; you walked in the midst of the stones of fire.*

But Lucifer's splendor and beauty did not last forever he got greedy and wanted more. Just like us, he had free will, he chose to act on his greed, and wickedness was found in him.

Ezekiel 28:15 - 17 – (NASB)
15 "You were blameless in your ways from the day you were created Until unrighteousness (wickedness) was found in you. 16 "By the abundance of your trade You were internally filled with violence, And you sinned; Therefore I have cast you as profane from the mountain of God. And I have destroyed you, O covering cherub, From the midst of the stones of fire. 17 "Your heart was lifted up because of your beauty; You corrupted your wisdom by reason of your splendor. I cast you to the ground; I put you before kings, that they may see you.

Lucifer wanted to overthrow the throne of God. As a highly exalted *created* being, he wanted to challenge God for His position. God took great care in providing Lucifer with great splendor – so much beauty and talent – that he considered his value equal to or even, above, God's. This led to a rebellion in heaven; war broke out. Lucifer, along with one-third of the angels, was hurled out of heaven.

Luke 10:18 – (NASB)
18 And He said to them, "I was watching Satan fall from heaven like lightning.

Revelation 12:3-4 7-9 - NASB
3 Then another sign appeared in heaven: and behold, a great red dragon having seven heads and ten horns, and on his heads were seven diadems. 4 And his tail swept away a third of the stars of heaven and threw them to the earth. And the dragon stood before the woman who was about to give birth, so

that when she gave birth he might devour her child.
⁷ And there was war in heaven, Michael and his angels waging war with the dragon. The dragon and his angels waged war, ⁸ and they were not strong enough, and there was no longer a place found for them in heaven. ⁹ And the great dragon was thrown down, the serpent of old who is called the devil and Satan, who deceives the whole world; he was thrown down to the earth, and his angels were thrown down with him.

Now that I've established that Satan (Lucifer) and demons are supernatural spiritual beings that fell from grace, we can talk about what happened next and what it meant for mankind.

It is my belief that some sort of metamorphosis happened to those who were "hurled" out of heaven. I believe that they became the four categories of beings listed in Ephesians 6:12.

> *Ephesians 6:11-12 – (NASB)*
> *¹¹ Put on the full armor of God, so that you will be able to stand firm against the schemes of the devil. ¹² For our struggle is not against flesh and blood, but against the rulers, against the powers, against the world forces of this darkness, against the spiritual forces of wickedness in the heavenly places.*

This is the platform from which I start my discussion of holy and fallen angels. From this point I will call the fallen angels demons.

DEMONS

I have taught Spiritual Warfare in our ministry for over 30 years. Among those who accept the existence of demons, there are various views as to their origin.

From my research I have identified four popular theories concerning the origin of demons.
    a) Theory 1 - Disembodied spirits
    b) Theory 2 –Offspring of wicked angels and women
    c) Theory 3 - Satan's creation
    d) Theory 4 - Fallen Angels

Theory 1: *Disembodied spirits* are those that use to dwell in human bodies, and now roam about without form. There are two schools of thought about this theory.

> Thought One: At another place and time, these demons existed in bodily form previous to mankind, as we know it. Even though the race died out, their spirits did not and have carried into our current era/age looking for new bodies.

> Thought Two: These spirits are from previous living humans that had unfinished business when on earth. They wait around inside a "holding place" until they finish their work. Once their business is completed they can continue on in their journey

This theory disregards the current relationship that God offers mankind. Our current spiritual reality has to do with our sin and the relationship with God, starting with Adam.

> *Romans 5:12 – (NASB)*
> *[12] Therefore, just as through one man sin entered into the world, and death through sin, and so death spread to all men, because all sinned—*

If there was a race before Adam the Bible is silent about it. Also when the spirit of a man leaves, it is to an external destination and not to roam about the earth, torment people or to have a role in earthly affairs. I know many people believe that people can talk to deceased relatives who want to get a message to their loved one. I know it is convincing, as they often do have information that only the dead and the living person knew. However, we know from the Biblical account of the rich man and Lazarus that the spirits of people who die have a destination to one of two places. They are not left to wander around until their unfinished business is completed.

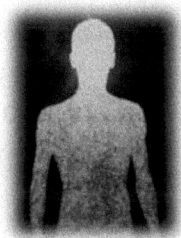

> *Luke 16:19-31 – (NASB)*
> *[19] "Now there was a rich man, and he habitually dressed in purple and fine linen, joyously living in splendor every day. [20] And a poor man named Lazarus was laid at his gate, covered with sores, 21 and longing to be fed with the crumbs which were falling from the rich man's table; besides, even the dogs were coming and licking his sores. [22] Now the poor man died and was carried away by the angels to Abraham's bosom; and the rich man also died and was buried. [23] In Hades he lifted up his eyes, being in torment, and *saw Abraham far away and Lazarus in his bosom. [24] And he cried out and said, 'Father Abraham, have mercy on me, and send Lazarus so that he may dip the tip of his finger in water and cool off my tongue, for I am in agony in this flame.' [25] But Abraham said, 'Child, remember that during your life you received your good things, and likewise Lazarus bad things; but now he is being*

comforted here, and you are in agony. ²⁶ And besides all this, between us and you there is a great chasm fixed, so that those who wish to come over from here to you will not be able, and that none may cross over from there to us.' ²⁷ And he said, 'Then I beg you, father, that you send him to my father's house— ²⁸ for I have five brothers—in order that he may warn them, so that they will not also come to this place of torment.' ²⁹ But Abraham *said, 'They have Moses and the Prophets; let them hear them.' ³⁰ But he said, 'No, father Abraham, but if someone goes to them from the dead, they will repent!' ³¹ But he said to him, 'If they do not listen to Moses and the Prophets, they will not be persuaded even if someone rises from the dead.'"

2 Corinthians 5:6-8 – (NASB)
⁶ Therefore, being always of good courage, and knowing that while we are at home in the body we are absent from the Lord ⁷ for we walk by faith, not by sight ⁸ we are of good courage, I say, and prefer rather to be absent from the body and to be at home with the Lord.

Theory 2: *Demons are the offspring* of an unnatural union between the *"sons of God"* (wicked angels) and the *"daughters of men"* (human women) recorded in Genesis 6.   Those who hold this belief, hypothesize that the children of this one-time union were wiped out in the flood and that their spirits became the demons.

Genesis 6:1-4 (NKJV)
¹ Now it came to pass, when men began to multiply on the face of the earth, and daughters were born to

them, ² that the sons of God saw the daughters of men, that they were beautiful; and they took wives for themselves of all whom they chose. ³ And the LORD said, "My Spirit shall not strive with man forever, for he is indeed flesh; yet his days shall be one hundred and twenty years." ⁴ There were giants on the earth in those days, and also afterward, when the sons of God came in to the daughters of men and they bore children to them. Those were the mighty men who were of old, men of renown.

Yet, just like with the pre-adamic demons, there is no mention in the Bible about the whereabouts of those offspring's. As the Bible is clear about the existence of both angels and demons, and their involvement with mankind, this interpretation of Genesis 6 also seems to imply that God somehow gave over mankind to be abused by wicked angels. This is difficult to believe and find that this passage is best left as a theological study rather than trying to explain demons.

Theory 3: Demons are Satan's Creations.

There is no reference in the Bible to indicate Satan has creation powers. Remember Satan is the great deceiver and wants us to think he can do more than he can. Creation is God's right and His right alone. I can't imagine what the state of this world would be if Satan had the power to create. He wants to corrupt, rob, steal and kill. (John 10:10) If he had the power to create our minds cannot conceive the wickedness that would be unleashed on our world.

Theory 4: Demons are Fallen Angels as a result of the rebellion in Heaven. This is the view most Christians subscribe

21

to. Demons were originally angels who fell from their holy state by committing sin against God. There is no specific date as to when this happened, but we do know Satan was ready to meet and deceive from the very beginning

Genesis 3 – (NASB)
³ Now the serpent was craftier than any beast of the field, which the Lord God had made. And he said to the woman, "Indeed, has God said, 'You shall not eat from any tree of the garden'?" ² The woman said to the serpent, "From the fruit of the trees of the garden we may eat; ³ but from the fruit of the tree which is in the middle of the garden, God has said, 'You shall not eat from it or touch it, or you will die.'" ⁴ The serpent said to the woman, "You surely will not die! ⁵ For God knows that in the day you eat from it your eyes will be opened, and you will be like God, knowing good and evil." ⁶ When the woman saw that the tree was good for food, and that it was a delight to the eyes, and that the tree was desirable to make one wise, she took from its fruit and ate; and she gave also to her husband with her, and he ate. ⁷ Then the eyes of both of them were opened, and they knew that they were naked; and they sewed fig leaves together and made themselves loin coverings. ⁸ They heard the sound of the Lord God walking in the garden in the cool of the day, and the man and his wife hid themselves from the presence of the Lord God among the trees of the garden. ⁹ Then the Lord God called to the man, and said to him, "Where are you?" ¹⁰ He said, "I heard the sound of you in the garden, and I was afraid because I was naked; so I hid myself." ¹¹ And He said, "Who told you that you

were naked? Have you eaten from the tree of which I commanded you not to eat?" 12 The man said, "The woman whom you gave to be with me, she gave me from the tree, and I ate." 13 Then the Lord God said to the woman, "What is this you have done?" And the woman said, "The serpent deceived me, and I ate." 14 The Lord God said to the serpent, "Because you have done this, Cursed are you more than all cattle, And more than every beast of the field; On your belly you will go, And dust you will eat All the days of your life; 15 And I will put enmity Between you and the woman, And between your seed and her seed; He shall bruise you on the head, And you shall bruise him on the heel." 16 To the woman He said, "I will greatly multiply Your pain in childbirth, In pain you will bring forth children; Yet your desire will be for your husband, And he will rule over you." 17 Then to Adam He said, "Because you have listened to the voice of your wife, and have eaten from the tree about which I commanded you, saying, 'You shall not eat from it'; Cursed is the ground because of you; In toil you will eat of it All the days of your life. 18 "Both thorns and thistles it shall grow for you; And you will eat the plants of the field; 19 By the sweat of your face You will eat bread, Till you -return to the ground, Because from it you were taken; For you are dust, And to dust you shall return." 20 Now the man called his wife's name Eve, because she was the mother of all the living. 21 The Lord God made garments of skin for Adam and his wife, and clothed them. 22 Then the Lord God said, "Behold, the man has become like one of Us, knowing good and evil; and now, he might stretch out his hand, and take also from the tree of life, and eat, and live forever"— 23 therefore the Lord

God sent him out from the garden of Eden, to cultivate the ground from which he was taken. 24 So He drove the man out; and at the east of the Garden of Eden He stationed the cherubim and the flaming sword, which turned every direction to guard the way to the tree of life

The Bible doesn't present all of the information in a chronological fashion. We are told to "study the Word" to understand its truths.

2 Timothy 2:15 – (NASB)
15 Be diligent to present yourself approved to God as a workman who does not need to be ashamed, accurately handling the word of truth.

Since the Bible does not tell the story of the fall of one-third of the angels in one single book of the Bible, we are left to interpret the scriptures. Revelation 12:4 is a great reference to the angels who fell with Satan.

Revelation 12:4 – (NASB)
4 And his tail *swept away a third of the stars of heaven and threw them to the earth. And the dragon stood before the woman who was about to give birth, so that when she gave birth he might devour her child.

By understanding the role angels have in heaven you can better grasp the diversity in the powers, responsibilities and functions of spiritual beings.

When thinking about God's original design of angels, we should consider the structure He put in place:

1. There is ranking, a system of authority between created beings

2. They were designed to be loyal and fulfill the Will of God

3. They had diverse abilities, functions and roles

Now I won't get any argument that angels watch over us; they give us messages, minister to us and keep us from harm. We should believe whole-heartedly that God uses angelic resources to protect mankind.   God's desire is that all mankind have a relationship with Him

> *2 Peter 3:9 - (NKJV)*
> *⁹ The Lord is not slack concerning His promise, as some count slackness, but is longsuffering toward us, not willing that any should perish but that all should come to repentance*

His desire is that none should perish.   Therefore, He assigns angels to care for His prized creation. Remember if one-third of the angels fell and became demons, two-third remain loyal unto God and committed to His Will.

> *Psalms 91:11-14 (NKJV)*
> *¹¹ For he will command his angels concerning you to guard you in all your ways; ¹² they will lift you up in their hands, so that you will not strike your foot against a stone.   ¹³ You will tread on the lion and the cobra; you will trample the great lion and the serpent. ¹⁴ "Because he loves me," says the Lord, "I will rescue him;   I will protect him, for he acknowledges my name.*

> *Daniel 10:10-15 (NKJV)*
> *¹⁰ A hand touched me and set me trembling on my hands and knees. ¹¹ He said, "Daniel, you who are highly esteemed, consider carefully the words I am*

about to speak to you, and stand up, for I have now been sent to you." And when he said this to me, I stood up trembling. ¹²Then he continued, "Do not be afraid, Daniel. Since the first day that you set your mind to gain understanding and to humble yourself before your God, your words were heard, and I have come in response to them. ¹³But the prince of the Persian kingdom resisted me twenty-one days. Then Michael, one of the chief princes, came to help me, because I was detained there with the king of Persia. ¹⁴Now I have come to explain to you what will happen to your people in the future, for the vision concerns a time yet to come." ¹⁵While he was saying this to me, I bowed with my face toward the ground and was speechless.

Hebrews 1:14 (NKJV)
¹⁴ "Are they not all ministering spirits, sent forth to minister for them who shall be heirs of salvation?"

Now if Angels watch over us, we can safely assume that demons also watch over us. Unfortunately, they don't have the same charge. Remember Satan's goals; to steal, kill and destroy.

John 10:10 - (NKJV)
¹⁰The thief does not come except to steal, and to kill, and to destroy. I have come that they may have life, and that they may have it more abundantly.

Satan is like a roaring lion seeking whom he can devour. (1Peter 5:8) Since that is his mission, I'm sure the ones that were 'hurled' with him are following the same path under Satan's leadership. After all, they were designed to be loyal, influential and to follow command of the one they serve.

1Peter 5:8 - (NKJV)
8 Be alert and of sober mind. Your enemy the devil prowls around like a roaring lion looking for someone to devour.

The Bible is clear that demons do exist. It is our job, as Christians, to study the word and grasp the fullness of its meaning.

2 Timothy 2:15 - (NKJV)
15 Be diligent to present yourself approved to God, a worker who does not need to be ashamed, rightly dividing the word of truth.

In fact, our ignorance determines the degree in which Satan is able to take advantage of us.

2 Corinthians 2:11- (KJV)
11 Lest Satan should get an advantage of us: for we are not ignorant of his devices.

The Bible talks about angels, holy and fallen, in military language and terminology. Among the terms used are the words "hosts" (1Kng.22: 19; Neh.9: 6; Dan.8: 10; cf. Lk.2: 13), "army" (Lk.2: 13; Rev.19: 9), "legion" (Matt.26: 53; Mk.5: 9; Lk.8: 30), and "band" (Ps.78: 49). Just as the Israelite assembly was called a warrior assembly (Num.chap.1-2; Deut.1: 15), so it is easy to assume that the angels would be characterized in the same way. God the Lord of the armies of Israel (Josh.5: 13-15; 1Sam.17: 45) and King of the nations (Job 12:23; Jer.18: 7-10), but He is also "Lord of Hosts", that is, commander of the angelic armies (e.g., Ps.84: 3; Is.6: 5;Am.5: 14-16; Zech.1: 3-17):I saw the Lord sitting on his throne with all the host of heaven standing around him on his right and his left. 1st Kings 22:19 [NIV]

You see this battle is not just between God and Satan. This battle is between them (Satan and demons) and us (God, Jesus, Holy Spirit, and mankind). Why do I believe this?

Ephesians 6:11-17 - (NASB)
[11] Put on the full armor of God, so that you will be able to stand firm against the schemes of the devil. [12] For our struggle is not against flesh and blood, but against the rulers, against the powers, against the world forces of this darkness, against the spiritual forces of wickedness in the heavenly places. [13] Therefore, take up the full armor of God, so that you will be able to resist in the evil day, and having done everything, to stand firm. [14] Stand firm therefore, having girded your loins with truth, ad having put on the breastplate of righteousness, [15] and having shod your feet with the preparation of the Gospel of peace; [16] in addition to all, taking up the shield of faith with which you will be able to extinguish all the flaming arrows of the evil one. [17] And take the helmet of Salvation and the sword of the Spirit, which is the word of God.

Not only does God tell us that the devil has 'wiles' (devious or cunning schemes employed in manipulating or persuading someone to do what one wants) but He lets us know who our enemy is and provides us with the necessary tools and weapons.

2 Corinthians 10:3-5 (NASB)
[3] For though we walk in the flesh, we do not war according to the flesh, [4] for the weapons of our warfare are not of the flesh, but divinely powerful for the destruction of fortresses. 5 We are destroying speculations and every lofty thing raised up against

the knowledge of God, and we are taking every thought captive to the obedience of Christ.

We are the prize for whoever wins the battle; and we have our part to play.   Both God and Satan have assigned spiritual beings to help or hurt us; guide us or deceive us, and ultimately win us over to an eternal cause.

For this reason, salvation plays a big part in spiritual assignments related to our lives.   If we haven't entered into a relationship with Jesus Christ, we allow Satan's forces far more influence than he should ever have. If we don't have our salvation, we subject ourselves to Satan's eternal will for us.

Romans 13:2 - (KJV)
2 Whosoever therefore resisteth the power resisteth the ordinance of God: and they that resist shall receive to themselves damnation.

There are two key foundational Christian concepts that must be understood before we talk further about man's role in spiritual warfare:

* Jesus is the Way, Truth and the Life and no man comes to God but by and through Him (John 14); Jesus gives us access to God and aligns us with His Will.
* God is Triune; the role of the Father, Son and Holy Spirit are distinct and effective in bringing forth salvation and victory in our lives (1 John 5)

When we become Christians, we join God's forces.   We have chosen to be on the side of goodness, truth and grace. To not choose means to allow Satan to influence against God. As you can see, mankind is in the middle of a tug-of-war and the battle wages on; the stage is set and continues to move toward the ultimate show down described in the Book of Revelation. God has His army and Satan has his army; both are fighting for us. God fights because He wants us; Satan fights because he wants to keep us from God. We are very important and were made to care for the world on God's behalf (Psalms 8, Genesis 1:26). Satan wants to ruin the legacy God created us to have.

Just by looking at the rankings of evil forces listed in Ephesians 6:12, we can assume that the Spiritual Wickedness in High Places is probably a category of wicked angels that hold the most power. The other three categories, Rulers of Darkness, Powers and Principalities roam the heavens and earth watching, waiting and creating havoc and unrest in response to Satan's bitter jealousy.

I use this diagram to illustrate Ephesians 6

God's Army	Satan's Army
God	
Jesus	
Holy Spirit	
Angels	Satan
Man	Spiritual wickedness in high places
	Rulers of darkness
	Powers
	Principalities

It is important to note where I put Satan and man in particular. Satan was and is, a fallen angel. His rank was similar to Michael and Gabriel, but with a different purpose. Satan is not equal to any member of the Godhead – the Father, Son or Holy Spirit.

Also, note that man is positioned to fight and overcome the spiritual forces pitted against us. How do we do that? Once we become Christians, the Holy Spirit is sealed in us.

> *Ephesians 1:13 - (NASB)*
> *[13] In Him, you also, after listening to the message of truth, the gospel of your salvation—having also believed, you were sealed in Him with the Holy Spirit of promise.*

We are given the power to overcome the world through the name and authority of Jesus and we have access to God through prayer.

> *Matthew 18:18-20 - (NASB)*
> *[18] Truly I say to you, whatever you bind on earth shall have been bound in heaven; and whatever you loose on earth shall have been loosed in heaven. [19] "Again I say to you, that if two of you agree on earth about anything that they may ask, it shall be done for them by My Father who is in heaven. [20] For where two or three have gathered together in My name, I am there in their midst."*

We are more than equipped for our role in the battle.

> *Philippians 2:9-11- (KJV)*
> *[9] Wherefore God also hath highly exalted him, and given him a name, which is above every name: [10]*

That at the name of Jesus every knee should bow, of things in heaven, and things in earth, and things under the earth; 11 And that every tongue should confess that Jesus Christ is Lord, to the glory of God the Father.

1 John 5:3-5 (KJV)
3 For this is the love of God, that we keep his commandments: and his commandments are not grievous. 4 For whatsoever is born of God overcometh the world: and this is the victory that overcometh the world, even our faith. 5 Who is he that overcometh the world, but he that believeth that Jesus is the Son of God?

2 Timothy 3:16-17 (NIV)
16 All Scripture is God-breathed and is useful for teaching, rebuking, correcting and training in righteousness, 17 so that the servant of God may be thoroughly equipped for every good work.

It is with this understanding, research and divine insight that I share my stories.

THREE

"SHE ANGEL" THE BEGINNING

Y ou might be asking yourself how a Christian woman, with my education and psychology background, believe in such "invisible" things. Well, it is my education (Biblical and academic) that has helped me understand my life experiences in a Christian context.

My relationship with a demon began at the age of two and ended when I was 20. It wasn't until much later that I understood this particular demon was a "familiar spirit", which was assigned to me for the purpose of keeping me from reaching my natural and spiritual potential.

A familiar spirit is a demon that has been assigned to get familiar with your life. Its job is to know your likes, ways, and habits; it can talk to other people about you and can talk to you about others. This is how spiritual understanding and information is often transferred into the physical world through mediums that might say they are talking with people that have died. Given what the Bible says about life after death, we know this is not true. This can entice you to follow after something other than Christ. Remember, we are the prize in this spiritual war and if Satan can get you to believe, and trust in something other than God, he's got your ear and that is how he got mine.

> Acts 16:16-21
> 16 It happened that as we were going to the place of prayer, a slave-girl having a spirit of divination met us,

33

who was bringing her masters much profit by fortune-telling. ¹⁷ Following after Paul and us, she kept crying out, saying, "These men are bond-servants of the Most High God, who are proclaiming to you the way of salvation." ¹⁸ She continued doing this for many days. But Paul was greatly annoyed, and turned and said to the spirit, "I command you in the name of Jesus Christ to come out of her!" And it came out at that very moment. ¹⁹ But when her masters saw that their hope of profit was gone, they seized Paul and Silas and dragged them into the market place before the authorities, ²⁰ and when they had brought them to the chief magistrates, they said, "These men are throwing our city into confusion, being Jews, ²¹ and are proclaiming customs which it is not lawful for us to accept or to observe, being Romans."

So, from scripture, we know that divination is real. Psychics and mediums can be "real" in the sense that they have spiritually-related information to share; yet Acts tells us to consider the *source* and not just the message. Many times the motivation behind the fortune telling is not of God.

This is my story

For as long as I can remember I had a reoccurring nightmare, which was the same every time I dreamed it. I would be wondering around in a forest trying to find my home. As I walked through the forest I would come to a clearing, which had a house in the middle of it. The front door would be open and I could see inside of the dark house. Once I stepped into the house I would be in a dark basement. A bit panicked by the fact that I couldn't see anything I would start searching for the light switch. I would find the switch, flip it on and find myself in a dimly lit daylight basement. As my eyes adjusted I could hear a rustling outside of the windows above my head. The rustling would turn to dragging footsteps. By this time I'm afraid. I would push myself against the wall, because I knew there was something outside looking for me. Slowly a figure would appear at the window to the right of me. The figure would stoop low to look through the window but thankfully they were frosted. The figure would try to wipe the frost off of the window but would give up and move to another window. Some of the windows were frosted and some were not. It would go from window to window trying to see in until it got to the window that was not frosted, which would be directly in front of me. It would stoop down and begin to wipe away the grime from the window. Just as it spotted me hiding in the corner I would wake up in a panic. This dream stopped when I was 20 years old.

The Beginning

I was very independent from a young age and I had a habit of leaving the house and wandering around my yard and always singing. You could say I was an "old soul" and a lot of my quirkiness was attributed to it.

I was sitting at the dining room table getting ready for dinner. There was a knock on the door. I went to the door and answered it. I have no answer as to why a two year old would be opening the door, but I did. I couldn't tell you what I saw but I do remember engaging in a conversation with whatever was at the door, letting it in my house and bringing it to the dinner table. My family didn't seem to notice anything unusual but my mom fussed at me for answering the door. So she asked me who was at the door. I told her nobody even though it was sitting right next to me. Thus began my relationship with the being I called "Porgy".

I talked to it, played with it and fought with it. I know my family tried to ignore my strange behavior because I was always a little quirky and old for my age. Finally it got to be too much for my mom and she asked who I was talking to. With Porgy's permission I told her. She looked at me, shook her head and walked out of the room.

My relationship with Porgy grew very strong, so strong that it concerned my dad, which in turn worried my mom. Up to that point, my mom shrugged off my quirkiness but when my dad got concerned it got her attention. They took me to a child psychiatrist who told them I was lonely and if they got me a dog my imaginary friend would go away. They got me a dog and Porgy went away...for about a year.

At the age of three, I now had a baby sister and a dog. Again, one night while at dinner, there was a knock on the door. My mom went to the door, came back and told my dad no one was there. They both decided it was kids playing a prank. Something inside of me quickened. I knew it wasn't a prank. I got up, ran to the door, opened it and yes you guessed it. There stood Porgy. It quickly stepped inside the house before my dad got to the door telling me to "get back to the dinner table". My mom asked me why I went to the door and I told her she left Porgy outside. I asked her to set a place at the table for "her". My parents looked at each other, my mom closed her eyes and shook her head. My sister started crying and life moved on.

From that point on she became part of our family. I say she because that is what I knew it was. It became easier to accept my "imaginary friend" because when I thought she was being ignored or mistreated I wasn't happy. Porgy was there to stay so no one challenged my thinking. That started a very dark clock ticking, as we had unknowingly accepted and given demonic influence a place in our home.

In the early years I didn't see a physical Porgy as much as I sensed her, but I knew she was present. She talked to me and told me information about people, most of which I didn't understand. She was my constant companion and the relationship with her became a normal part of our lives. When I began seeing her at the age of 8 it was no surprise to my mom but that was when my mom got really concerned but didn't know what to do.

Porgy manifested into a woman like figure draped in a grey cape with a hood. I could not see her face. When she manifested in her semi--physical form, she no longer came to the house, instead she stood off at a distance and watched. She was always present, everywhere I went; she was there in the background just watching.

By the time I was 10 my "knowing things" had increased and I knew that I had a special gift. My predictions were so accurate and consistent that my mother called me the "black gypsy" and the neighborhood knew I saw things. One afternoon I was washing dishes, as I stared into the soapy water, I saw the face of my Great Aunt. She looked at me and was mouthing words. When the face disappeared I knew my aunt was dead. I ran to my mom and told her that my aunt was dead. About 5 minutes later the phone rang and it was my mom's cousin telling her that her aunt was dead. I remember my mom turning and looking at me. She hung the phone up and shook her head. All she said to me was, "sometimes you scare me". That experience was another significant turning point in my life. I didn't want to scare my mom, but I liked the feeling I got from knowing things that others didn't know. From that point on, I wasn't shy about telling people what I knew. Kids from the neighborhood would run from me because they thought I would tell them that they were going to die but it also made me very popular.

The "power" of the influence began to grow and with it, so did the manifestation of Porgy. I remember playing tag one evening. I ran around the back of the house, it was dusk and I knew Porgy was looking at me. I turned my head to the right and there she was standing in the distance watching. I could not see her face, but I wasn't afraid and I wasn't surprised. She was part of my life and it just seemed to "make sense" to see more of her. This time however, instead of just passively watching me, she beckoned me. Focused on her, I started towards her, but just then one of my friends tagged me out. That turned my attention back towards the game; the moment was broken. Around the age of 11 a neighbor girl introduced me to the Ouija board. I was fascinated by it and wanted to see how it worked but I was also afraid of it. Somehow I had learned that it was evil. This was the first sense of "ill" I had about spiritual things, but I still had no sense that Porgy was anyone or anything bad. She just was there, and she was mine – and that made it feel like a good thing. However, it appeared that I wasn't going to be allowed to just let things be. I was being pushed and pulled by people and forces to take just one more step into spiritual things. I would go to my friend's house and play around with the board. It was no big deal. We would laugh and move the dial spelling words that we made up. It was harmless, or so I thought.

One day while I was at my house watching Bewitched a few of the neighborhood girls came to my screen door and asked me if I wanted to come do a séance with them. I said no (I didn't know what a séance was but it didn't sound fun). They begged and begged until I gave in. They told me I was the only one who had the real power and they wanted to "talk to the spirits". I hadn't ever really considered *initiating* conversation with spirits, but thought this might be a good time to see if I could get more information about people. We headed over to my friend's house because her parents weren't home and my mom would have choked me for bringing "that devil stuff" in her house. But oh how I wished I had listened to my mom and left that "devil stuff" alone.

We went to her downstairs bedroom. I felt excited - like something big was going to happen. My friend put the game on the bed we all sat on the bed. I was put in charge of the game. We played around with it for about 15 minutes calling out names and summoning demons. We laughed and mocked and thought we were having a great time until the board began to spell out words. Now I knew something had taken control of the board but the girls thought it was me entertaining them. So they became more and more excited as the words became sentences. We used that board for several hours. I was the only one who knew that something else had moved the dial. I kept it to myself and felt a tingle of excitement. I looked around several times to see if Porgy was there, but she never came.

Arriving home from our evening of fun, there she was in the distance watching. She had accomplished one of her goals; getting me interested in the things of the occult and I liked the feeling.
A few weeks later a group of neighbor kids came and got me. The news had spread like wildfire that I could "make

the board talk" and they wanted to see me work the board. I wasn't really sure what had happened weeks earlier but I liked the attention so I went with them. This time there were too many kids to come into the house so my friends worked out a rotation system to watch the show. Once we were settled in, they wanted me to call up spirits from the dead and have them visit us. I wasn't sure I wanted to do that, because something inside of me knew that couldn't be good. Even though I shook my head and told them I didn't think that was a good idea, they begged and begged and begged. So, with a little reluctance I agreed. After all, I was a little curious myself. I touched the board and asked for any spirits that could hear my voice to come into the room. In retrospect, I often wonder how I knew to say that. It was as if my mind was infused with insight. It was a natural request given the progression of my spiritual conversations and experiences at the time.

To my right was my eight year old sister and to my left, my friend. There was about a foot between my friend and me. The dial began to move, slowly at first and then rapidly. It spelled out a name which none of us could pronounce but what we could read was that it was there in the room with us.

Slowly a depression formed in the bed between my friend and me. It looked as if someone was sitting on the bed but we couldn't see it. That was bad enough but an eerie cold fear crept into the room. My friend froze and tried to scream but no sound came out of her mouth. The look on her face got the attention of the others in the circle. My friend's reaction got everyone's attention. They looked at me, I don't know what my face was doing but it also got their attention. The girls came around to our side of the bed to see what we were looking at. They froze for a few seconds. Then, the fear struck all of us at the same moment. Screams rang out like a loud siren and we went running out of the house. We ran past the kids that were waiting for their turn to get in the house. When they saw us running they started running also. I out ran everyone else, all the while hoping that the evil didn't follow me home. I ran into the house, slammed the door and sat down on the couch. I was so scared that I didn't realize I had left my eight-year old sister to fend for herself. My mom came out of the kitchen after hearing the door slam and saw me sitting on the couch watching TV. She knew something was up because there was a gardening show on the T.V. and I was looking at it like it was the best show on earth. That didn't fool my mom; she asked me what I was doing in the house in the middle of the day watching a gardening show. I ignored her. That was very unusual for me to ignore her. I was a very obedient and responsible child. I was the oldest of four and had to help my mom. My dad was in the Air Force and gone overseas a lot. My mom went to school and worked full time. Knowing how out of character it was for me to ignore her she asked me what happened and where was my sister. I couldn't ignore her anymore and hesitantly told her what happened. She sternly reminded me that she had told me not to mess with "that stuff" and she was glad I got the mess scared out of me, hoping that maybe now I would leave it alone. She walked out of the room. Yelling back into the living room she said, "You better go find your sister".

Getting up from the couch I was returning to myself but also feeling a little confused. How could my gift create such evil? And how could that evil, after the fear wore off, make you even more curious? I stepped outside of the door and looked down the side of my house. You guessed it; Porgy was standing in her familiar spot. This time, however, I could see the outline of her face. It was as if she had a transparent veil over her face, but it was distinguishable nonetheless. Just then my sister came running down the hill. She was angry with me for leaving her. She had fallen down and was stepped on by several girls trying to get out of the house. Her knee was scraped, her lip was bloody and she was sobbing. I felt horrible but didn't want my mom to find out what happened. So I quickly brought her into the house, took her to our room and cleaned her up. I calmed her down and got her distracted by playing with our Barbie dolls. By the time my mom came to check on us my sister was back to normal. She did tell my mom what happened, but she really didn't understand the magnitude of the situation. I was glad. She was scared because the girls were screaming. She didn't see the depression in the bed so when the girls started running she ran to. I told her we were playing a game and we were trying to scare each other. My mom gave me another lecture about taking care of my baby sister and she hoped I learned my lesson. I did learn my lesson; I wasn't going to take my sister with me anymore. I don't think that was the lesson my mom wanted me to learn.

This presented me with a major moment of choice. I understood the power of my gift and the fear it brought but I didn't understand that exercising this gift was bringing my longtime friend, Porgy, closer and closer to me. Neither scenario was good but I didn't know this. Unfortunately that kept me connected to a spiritual realm that was not willing to give me up and was willing to do and use anything and anyone to keep me in blindness. The next day the girls and I made a promise to never touch the Ouija board again. However, in the corner of my heart I had a feeling I was not going to keep that promise. From that day forward, the entire neighborhood gave me a lot of respect and my curiosity grew more and more each day. When someone wanted to know something they came to me. Sometimes I had the information and sometimes I didn't. I never made things up because the irony of it was that I went to church and was very interested in God. I knew it wasn't right to lie.

My parents didn't attend church, but they made sure we were in Sunday service and participated in everything the church had to offer. The church influence I did have at the time provided me with my moral compass and the little bit of caution that I always felt but disregarded. God was doing his part to reclaim me well before I could understand what this was really all about.

At church, there was one woman who took me under her wing and poured into me until I graduated from high school. Her name was Ms. Steel. I knew Ms. Steel loved me. I would get so mad at her because she would make our class memorize scriptures. It was the memorization of those scriptures that would later save my spiritual life. I credit her for establishing my spiritual foundation. Even with all the love, kindness and support I received at church, no one knew anything about what I was experiencing. There was no mention of the devil, other than he was the bad guy and there was certainly no mention of demons. I was told to not talk about that "stuff" because it would scare people. I didn't know what Ms. Steel's beliefs were about angels and demons but I do think she knew I had insight into spiritual things that weren't normal. I remember one day her telling me; "You are a very gifted young lady. You will go far, and be very successful. Make sure you use all of those gifts for God and don't let anything pull you off of your path with

43

God." It was the way she said it that made such a lasting impression in my mind. I later on had the blessing of meeting and befriending her great-granddaughter. I was able to share my story with her and tell her how thankful I was for having her great-grandmother in my life. Even though I couldn't really explore the spirit realm with Ms. Steel, she let me experience the full and lasting impact of Christ's love. This became my anchor that helped me discern between true love, and Satan's deception later in life.

If I may digress a little, it is imperative that youth ministries are seen as a priority for churches. You never know who you are ministering to. Every child has a story and a destiny. Just like me, it just might be a future Pastor's wife who was headed for a life on the dark side.

Through my growing relationship with God, I decided to leave the Ouija board alone and not call any more spirits to come and visit. I didn't like the fear and cold that I felt. I knew that feeling was very bad and directly opposed to the feelings that I experienced at church. But there was another force that kept me away from the board, as well - my mom. She put the fear of God in me by telling me that if I kept messing with that board something would come and get me in the night. It kept me away from the board all right but it scared me so bad I couldn't sleep at night. Talk about needing to be careful about what you say to kids. To combat my fear, I had a ritual prayer I said every night.

> Now I lay me down to sleep,
> I pray the Lord my soul to keep
> If I should die before I wake,
> I pray the lord my soul to take.

Many children have nightly prayers, but in my case I fully believed at age 11 that this prayer was the only thing keeping the evil away from me. I would wake up in the middle of the night in a cold sweat if I forgot to say that prayer. You see, I didn't know God had his own forces, such as my guardian angels, watching over me to keep evil at bay. All I remember was the experience in the bedroom several months earlier and I didn't want any more experiences like that. As I thought more and more about God, Porgy's influences lessened, but did not completely disappear.

At the age of 12 I was setting in church listening to the Pastor. What an oxymoron I was. I was so enticed by spiritual things, yet confused about what was good, right, holy or evil. I considered Porgy a friend and felt "at home" with both her and Ms. Steel. I felt like I was in a place between two spiritual forces, although I would have never said it that way at the time. However, at the end of his sermon, when Pastor offered salvation, a surge went through me like a warm lightning bolt. I shot out of my seat grabbed my sister's hand and up we went. I responded to the beckoning of God.

I accepted the Lord, as my savior and it was a glorious day. Ms. Steel had a done an excellent job getting me to the foot of the Cross; I know she prayed for me. I could see her face beaming as I was baptized that evening. It is still to this day one of the most memorable events in my life.

So here I was a child of God by choice and at the same time I was involved with a being that was not of the Lord. How could a born again believer still be attached to a demon? The operative word is attached. I wasn't possessed

45

but this being was assigned to me probably from birth. I had to at some point denounce it. Both God and Satan were fighting for me. I was afraid, excited and curious at the same time. That is how I entered my teenage years.

MIDDLE AND HIGH SCHOOL

My dad was stationed in Illinois at the end of my 6th grade year. Moving to another state and a new school was hard enough but I also realized that once we moved out of Washington, I no longer saw Porgy. I was too busy fighting and trying to stay alive. It was the first time I was consumed with the physical world, without Porgy's companionship. We didn't go to church so my Christian walk was halted. Life without Porgy created a vacuum that I filled with ungodly things. Coming from a non-violent environment to a violent poverty stricken neighborhood was so traumatic. I saw, did and heard things that never crossed my mind until we moved there. I guess Porgy didn't have to be there; I was doing badly all by myself. I didn't have anyone in Illinois to help me understand the need to willingly give up old things to make room for God's presence to grow in me. I didn't have anyone to tell me that God was always with me, and He would never forsake me. I felt all alone.

2 Corinthians 7:1 (NIV)
7 Therefore, since we have these promises, dear friends, let us purify ourselves from everything that contaminates body and spirit, perfecting holiness out of reverence for God.

James 4:8 – (NIV)
8 Come near to God and he will come near to you. Wash your hands, you sinners, and purify your hearts, you double-minded.

Deuteronomy 31:6 - (NASB)
⁶Be strong and courageous, do not be afraid or tremble at them, for the LORD your God is the one who goes with you. He will not fail you or forsake you."

We moved back to Washington a year later. I was now 13. Guess who greeted me in our new house?   You got it, Porgy. Because I hadn't filled the void of my friendship with her with a strong relationship with God, I quickly fell into old habits. I was happy to see her because I had unanswered questions about things and she had always been the source I turned to for knowledge. The demonic experience in the bedroom the year before, still puzzled me. The fear of it had moved me toward God but I hadn't resolved how I was able to make it happen. I was hoping Porgy could give me some answers and teach me about what had happened. And with that thought, I went sliding down a dark slippery slope. Porgy had done her job. She got me to feel proud about my "gift" and curious about the evil I had conjured up. When I returned to her, she helped me explore the answers I sought.   I was never afraid of her. I accepted who I was and what I could do just as someone would accept a singing voice as a unique talent. When I would look she was there. Even when I didn't see her I knew she was there because I could sense her presence; it was comforting. I gained strength from her. I got messages from her. I knew things about people and began to use it to control people. I liked the power. I felt like this was who I was made to be.

Yet, along with this increase of darkness around me, the Holy Spirit and God's angels were also working to move me closer to God.   I had a teacher in the 8th grade that took me under her wing. She saw my potential and kept me involved in school activities. She also encouraged me to go back to church, which I did.

So, here I was, a Christian trying to grow in God while playing with "powers of darkness." I continued my dual spiritual journey for another seven years.   During those years, I went to church and dabbled in the dark arts. I had no idea that what I was doing was not a part of Jesus. I knew God was spiritual. I knew about faith and I figured if God gave me these gifts, I should be using them. My mistake was repeatedly turning, to Porgy, a demonic force, to explain to me how to use those gifts. I thought the more I used them, the more I would come to understand why I had them – why God gave them to me.

Even with my curiosity and my voracious appetite for reading books about ESP, Telekinesis, Clairvoyance, Astro-projection, I wasn't comfortable with the evil presence I felt when I practiced these "arts". I lived with a dilemma.   When I tried to understand and use my gifts, under Porgy's direction and knowledge I got from the books I read, the worse I felt. The sense of darkness and evil couldn't be shaken. I had enough Jesus in me to never be comfortable with these practices, and that was what kept me from fully embracing the occult world that I seemed to have an aptitude for. I was not a witch; I didn't take a pledge of allegiance or participate in anything that I thought was blatantly anti-God.   I was a misguided young woman who had wonderful gifts from God, which Satan tried to steal for his use. The problem wasn't with my spiritual understanding; it was with my use of the spiritual knowledge I had. It was with my motivations and where I turned to understand myself as a unique creation. If I wanted to know about my God-given talent then I needed to seek answers exclusively from the one who made me in my mother's womb.

Psalm 139:14 – (NIV)
14 I praise you because I am fearfully and wonderfully made; Your works are wonderful, I know that full well.

My angels watching over me kept me in check during this period of time and for that I am grateful. The Holy Spirit in me, although grieved, provided me with a sense of boundary that I could not cross.

Ephesians 1:13 - (NIV)
13 And you also were included in Christ when you heard the message of truth, the gospel of your salvation. When you believed, you were marked in him with a seal, the promised Holy Spirit.

FOUR

"SHE ANGEL" - THE END

My high school years were filled with living on the edge of God and Satan's battle over me and my gifts. While I was trying to deal with understanding my choice in the middle of it all, my family had to deal with the demonic presence in our house.

It didn't take long for everyone in the family to agree that our house was "haunted." It was normal to be awakened at 3 or 4am by footsteps coming up the stairs. My siblings would get me up to go and see who it was. We all creped down the stairs, me in front, my sister next and our 2 younger brothers behind her. As we got down to the bottom of the steps we never found anyone. As soon as we went back to our rooms, the footsteps would start again. The manifestations were so frequent we finally ignored them.

We got use to the doors slamming, the lights turning on and off and the footsteps at night. However one particular disturbance started the last two years of high school and stopped when I went to college. The disturbance always happened in a room upstairs. We lived in a house about 100 years old. It had a lot of character. There was one room we called our "kids" room. It was located off of the bathroom and at the end of the hallway from our bedrooms. For many years the room was used as a storage room, a messy storage room. It never crossed our minds that the room could be used for anything other than a storage room. One day I decided to turn that room into a room we could use. I talked my siblings into helping me and we worked the entire day cleaning and decorating. By that evening, our "kids" room was perfect. We had a couple of throw rugs, 3 large pillows, and lamps around the ledges, a record player and radio. It was heaven. We would spend hours in that room. One of my favorite things to do would be to go into the room shut the door read and listen to music. It was my safe haven.

For about 2 weeks it was perfect until one Saturday morning. I headed to the room to read and to listen to music. As I approached the room I felt a strange sensation come over me. It felt like a caution light had gone off in my soul. It had been a long time since I had seen Porgy that I almost forgot that foreboding feeling. I opened the door stepped into the room and what I saw took my breath away. The room was totally destroyed. The lamps were knocked off the ledge; pillows and records were on the floor. The record player was turned upside down and the rugs were thrown around. I was dumbfounded and for a quick second I acknowledged that whatever did this was not human. I immediately shut that down. I told myself I was being irrational, that one of my siblings had done this as a joke. So I got furious because I had just spent an hour the night before making sure the room was clean so I could use it the next day. I hauled my siblings into the room and started to fuss until I noticed the looks of puzzlement on their faces. I asked them if they had done that to the room and they all said no and I believed them. They helped me clean it up and I listened to music and read my book. I shrugged it off as my dad's attempt at a joke or some sort of punishment. I left the room that night neat and tidy and a little concerned.

The next day was Sunday and I headed to the room to do homework. I opened the door and yep you guessed it the room was disrupted again. This time I knew it wasn't a sick joke, or some form of punishment. One side of me believed it had to be one of my brothers but another thought was starting to emerge in the corner of my mind that the culprit was not human. Once again I hauled my siblings up the stairs and questioned them. For the second time they all denied having any involvement in the destruction of the room. In fact they all said they had not even went into the room for a couple of days. I knew that to be true, because the room had gotten boring to them and I was typically the only one that used it. So I had my dad put a dead bolt on the room, I was determined to prove that one of them was responsible for the mess.

The next day after school I was anxious to see what the room looked like. I unlocked the door and stepped in the room. There was no denying it, no human was involved. I went in the room and began cleaning it. I never felt the same about the room from that time on. In fact no one stayed in that room alone and we always had to straighten it up in the mornings. Eventually we stopped using the room, took the items out and locked the door.

At the height of these disturbances I once again had another spiritual epiphany. I was asleep, my back was to the door and a cold demonic air awakened me in my room. As the sleepiness cleared from my mind I realized *It* was in my room. At first fear gripped me like sleeping in a too tight sleeping bag. I felt suffocated and panic rose up inside of me. My mind flipped all over the place and I felt like *It* would take me over. I had a fleeting realization that I was in the company of the same thing that sat next to me in the séance six years earlier. I was confused but I knew *It* was not good. Searching my mind for what to do, I heard a small voice tell me to say "Jesus". That command quieted me long enough for me to collect myself and out of my core a fury rose up in me. I turned around, got out of bed and yelled "get out of my room in Jesus name!" As soon as the words left my mouth, the room returned to normal and It was gone. That really stunned me. It was the first time I used Jesus as a way to protect me. It also confused me. How could I conjure up evil and then also make it go away? It filled me with a sense of power and peace to know that I could control them, but I still did not fully understand the spiritual implications.

From that point on, I knew I could keep demons out of my room, at least when I was there (even if the rest of the house was a free for all). I wish I could have seen the angels that God put outside my door to keep those demons at bay. From this experience, I figured out how to find a little space of peace and to manage the spirits. I also, for the first time began to understand that there might be two types of spiritual beings – good and evil, angels and demons.

Two months later, I was again sleeping and this time a presence entered my room, it did not bring cold air, it did not feel threatening and I was not afraid. In fact, it brought such a peace and stillness that I wanted to lay very still and enjoy every moment. She began to speak to me. She told me about my future, my husband and my career. I was 16 years old. I had my first "Angelic" visitation from my Lord and Savior. That experience was so profound that to this day I remember it like it was yesterday. Oh by the way everything that angel told me came to pass, including writing this book.

The next significant turning point in my journey came in my sophomore year of college. The experience of my angelic visitation was still a forward memory but a slight veil had slipped over my eyes. I now had a good understanding of both sides but I had no spiritual education to help me understand what they were both all about. It was once again a fight for me. I was sitting in the front row enjoying the show of a famous magician who came to campus. I always loved magicians. I was intrigued by their gifts. One trick performed that night was to place a number in an envelope and implant that number in someone's head. As I watched him work the trick, a red number lit up in my head. It burned in my mind like a branding iron burns a mark in the side of a cow. He asked for the person who got the number to come to the front. So, there I went with all eyes staring at me. It never occurred to me that I could be wrong; I had a number burning in my head and I was intrigued. As I walked forward a million questions ran through my head right along with the red number. The biggest one was HOW DID HE DO THAT??!??! What gift did he have that allowed him to put that number in my head? I got to the front and told him the number. The magician opened the sealed envelope and, you guessed it, it was the same number. I knew then that I was truly gifted. I wanted to be able to do something like that. I was hooked again. My angels had to be shaking their heads. Unfortunately, I was not attending church and was fully involved in college behavior. I was once again vulnerable. Not moving forward with God left me vulnerable to the familiar influences that enticed me since I was two.

My natural "wiring" is to question why and how things happened. So that show got me thinking. Since I had gifts, shouldn't I try and see where they could take me. I jumped into research and came upon information regarding Para-psychology. What a coincidence! I was a psychology major and wanted to understand the brain, maybe I was meant to have a career in explaining the paranormal. I sent off for information. A week later materials came in my mailbox and one of the colleges caught my attention. It actually jumped off the page, like the number in my head. It was an advertisement for a college in California that specialized in Para-psychology. I thought this must have been the hand of fate. After all, God gave me this gift and I could use it for Him professionally. By now, I had decided that my gifts were from God because they were so unique. And with these materials in hand, I felt as if He was directing my path. What really sealed the deal was that it was a Spanish speaking college and I was a Spanish minor. "Amazing!" I thought, "Look how God pointed me to the right school!" It was the perfect set up. I could go down during our winter interim term and if I liked it I could possibly transfer. I was so excited, because I could practice telekinesis, clairvoyance and ESP. Things I had "a gift" for. What a gift I was given, I could go to college get extra credit and figure out how to use my abilities for good.

So off to California I want to study Para-psychology. I thought this was a blessing from God but in reality it was the culminating point of my dark journey. What Satan intends for evil, God can use for good.

I truly understand the scriptures below because they have gotten me through many things. Just like Joseph, who had a great destiny, that led him through slavery, false accusations and imprisonment, I had to be tested. Joseph learned through his journey, so that at the right time, he had the knowledge and ability to accomplish what God intended all along.

> *Genesis 50:18-21 (NIV)*
> *18 His brothers then came and threw themselves down before him. "We are your slaves," they said. 19 But Joseph said to them, "Don't be afraid. Am I in the place of God? 20 You intended to harm me, but God intended it for good to accomplish what is now being done, the saving of many lives. 21 So then, don't be afraid. I will provide for you and your children." And he reassured them and spoke kindly to them.*

The time in California led to my awakening. It lead me to find the Truth as only God can provide. God intended it for good to accomplish what is now being done, the saving of many lives, in and through my counseling and ministry.

> *Isaiah 59:19*
> *19 So shall they fear the name of the Lord from the west, and His glory from the rising of the sun; When the enemy comes in like a flood, The Spirit of the Lord will lift up a standard against him.*

> *Romans 8:28*
> *28 And we know that all things work together for good to those who love God, to those who are the called according to His purpose.*

I was following the path my familiar spirit had planned for me. Porgy's, goal was to take me from God. The plan was to take all I was purposed for away, by enticing me just like the Serpent enticed Eve with the fruit (Genesis 3 earlier quoted). It was something that could be considered innocent and satisfying, but it was eaten outside the Will of

God. When actions are separated from God, they become sin and sin does nothing but kill the soul.

But God also had a plan; He knew the moment my understanding would finally yield unto Him. I knew my angels were with me all along, they were anticipating the break through when I would finally let go of evil attachments and serve God fully. I wonder from time to time what the conversations were like during those times; the strategizing as the moment of truth grew near. Each camp was positioning itself for the final strike; to claim me. I had no idea what was getting ready to happen to me, but God did.

I loved the school and was very successful. I led my classes in all of the experiments and displayed extraordinary gifts. I was comfortable using my talents, but also knew what the "bad" felt like. So when I would begin to feel the bad feelings associated with the experimentation, I would stop. Porgy was ever present; she always brought me back to the next enticement, or gave a false sense of control and security. The strategy was very clever. You see, even though I had been a Christian for eight years, I still had no idea that what I was doing wasn't of God. The deception was reinforced. The familiar spirit was using my God given gifts to lure me away from my original purpose, which was to serve God and His people with a sensitivity and understanding of spiritual influence.

It was in this setting, when I was closest to being lost, that my angels put their plan into action.

I was sitting in my only non-Spanish speaking class. We were studying hypnosis. The professor wanted to demonstrate to the class what a person acted like when they were placed in a hypnotic trance. He explained that people have access to parts of their brains that they typically don't use.

With that short introduction he asked for a volunteer. The class nominated a shy and reserve student named Sam as a joke. He asked Sam if he was comfortable with the class's decision. He seemed a bit reluctant but smiled as he said yes.

It only took a few minutes and Sam was in the hypnotic trance. The professor told him in Spanish that I had his belly button. Sam got out of his seat, walked over to me and demanded in Spanish the return of his belly button. Stunned, I managed to tell him I didn't have it. That only angered him because he believed if he didn't get his belly button back, his insides would come out. Of course, I didn't know his fear at the time, so I just kept repeating, with a smile, that I didn't have it. The more I insisted that I didn't have it, the angrier he got. By the fourth denial Sam was desperate. I realized when he came after me that this no longer was a game. I got out of my seat and ran out of the room. Sam ran after me and kept repeating in Spanish, "let me look for it, I know you have it."

I could hear my professor and the students laughing because they all thought it was an act. When I didn't stop, Sam told me in Spanish he was going to kill me if I didn't give him his belly button back. Running down the hallway, I decided to stop and tell him I was done. When, I slowed down and turned, I realized Sam wasn't Sam anymore. Something had taken him over. What I saw in his eyes told me he wasn't playing. It caused a fear I had never experienced before. A shot of adrenaline raced through my body and I took off like I was running the 440 in the Olympics. Now I've never been a fast runner, but I ran like a gazelle. It's amazing what you can make your body do when you are running for your life! The college was a beautifully restored 100-year-old building. The ceilings were high, the hallways were long and the lighting was low. Just the right combination for a horror movie only it wasn't a movie. The faster I ran, the faster Sam yelled and cussed right behind me. He kept saying his insides were coming out. Adrenaline started to dissipate and I slowed down. I knew I had to find a hiding place. I could hear my professor yelling at Sam telling him that was enough and leave me alone but Sam was on a mission. I spotted a doorway with a deep inset. I thought I could get in there, cover up and stave him off until someone came to help me. I darted into the deep door-well and tried to open the door but it was locked. By this time I could hear the footsteps of people running in my direction. Everyone was telling Sam to stop and leave me alone. Sam reached the door opening and grabbed my shirt, searching for his belly button. He ripped at my clothes while choking me. I was screaming and yelling for help, while slapping and pushing his hands in an attempt to keep him from stripping and choking me. I thought "Jesus, please don't let this man strip me naked in this corner in front of everyone!" I saw spots and the walls were moving, I knew I would be unconscious any minute. Finally, two football players made it to the door grabbed Sam and threw him to the ground. He was frantic and out of control. In order to keep him from getting to me, it took two more football players to subdue him. They pinned him to the floor while the professor took him out of the trance.

They brought Sam back to class and put him in his seat. My professor apologized for what happened. He said it wasn't supposed to happen that way. He didn't know what had gotten into Sam who was normally a shy and quiet young man. I could hear comments made by the other students who were surprised at Sam's actions. They said he was acting like a mad man, like something took him over. Sam was dazed and confused. He wasn't aware of anything that had happened. He was desperately trying to collect himself. He noticed his torn shirt, bloody lip and knot on his forehead, which he had gotten when thrown to the ground. He asked what happened. The professor in great detail told the story. Sam looked at me with horror in his face, apologizing over and over again and shaking his head. I, on the other hand, was not dazed or confused; just scared. That was the first time I ever saw a possession. I sat in my seat and adjusted my clothes. I knew something took over Sam and I didn't want to see it again.

I went home that day feeling uncomfortable about the day's event. I knew the implications were much bigger than an "out of control belly button episode". Something deep within my spirit started to stir. It was like flickers of light welling up in me. For the first time, I questioned whether the 'stuff' I was doing was right. I couldn't or wouldn't allow this to go unanswered, and I began to understand that the answers I had received before could not be trusted.

The next day when I walked into class I could cut the tension with a knife. I certainly didn't want to go through class knowing things were unresolved. So I approached Sam. I wanted to tell him how cool I thought it was that we were the only students who spoke Spanish. I also thought it was a nice segue into a conversation about the incident. So I said in Spanish that I had no hard feelings about the day before. Sam responded with a puzzled look on his face. He smiled and shook his head yes.

I went back to my seat and sat down confused about his reaction. The student in front of me turned around and said.

"Sam doesn't speak Spanish." I said "but" the student shook his head comprehending what we had both witnessed the day before. He turned around and went silent. I looked at Sam. He shrugged his shoulders and we all sat in silence for the rest of the class. Needless to say our professor didn't put anyone else in a hypnotic trance for the rest of our class.

About a week later, things became even more disturbing when a body was found in the ravine across the street from our complex. The police were going door to door informing us that the killer had been spotted in our area and keep stay inside and keep our doors locked.

As I thought about what happened in class, the murder, and my increase awareness of my "supernatural" gifts, it felt like a veil began to lift from my eyes. The more it lifted the more uncomfortable I got with what I was into and where I was. I wish I could have seen what was going on in the spirit realm. I believe my angels finally had permission to allow me to slowly see what my familiar spirit (demon) had planned for me. This revelation was crucial and timely.

> 2 Corinthians 10:5 (NIV)
> 5 We demolish arguments and every pretension that sets itself up against the knowledge of God, and we take captive every thought to make it obedient to Christ.

> Colossians 1:9-10 (NIV)
> 9 For this reason, since the day we heard about you, we have not stopped praying for you. We continually ask God to fill you with the knowledge of his will through all the wisdom and understanding that the Spirit gives, 10 so that you may live a life worthy of the

61

Lord and please him in every way: bearing fruit in every good work, growing in the knowledge of God,

That evening I prayed, "Lord if you get me out of here, I will never dabble in this "stuff' again". I felt really scared for the first time. Thank God the interim was almost over. I tossed and turned half way through the night. I had a lot on my mind. I laid in bed running all the different experiences I had since I had come to California. Then I reflected on my past, Porgy, the séance and my gifts. It all ran together like the closing credits of a movie. I had an important meeting in the morning to discuss my transfer to the school. I was such a good student, they wanted me to transfer at the beginning of spring semester and continue my studies. I drifted off to sleep. Around 1:00am, a chill in the room woke me. I thought the window was left opened and told myself I had better get up and close it, after all there was a killer loose and I didn't want him having access to our apartment through an open window. I tried to shake the sleepy webs out of my mind because I felt like I was still dreaming. The room was extremely cold, a cold deeper than I had never felt. I also noticed a light smoke or haze in the room. I looked over at my roommate and she was fast asleep. As I scanned the room, I felt the familiar bad feeling. The one I got when I knew something evil was getting ready to happen. I could feel the hair on my arms stand straight up. I knew this was not good. Then, slowly, Porgy appeared in front of my closet door. It was the first time I had seen her in solid form. But there was no mistaking it was she. I thought I was dreaming so I tried to shake sleep off of me and re-focus. The second time I looked in her direction made me know, without a doubt, that I wasn't dreaming and that she was really there. I was terrified, but why? All of my life she was with me and I never feared her, but that night she brought with her a presence that was not peaceful, calming or comfortable. Words cannot describe the fear I felt. I was so afraid that I couldn't speak, I tried to wake up my roommate but nothing would come out of my mouth. The more I tried to speak the colder the room got and the more terrified I became. Then she stretched out her hand and beckoned me. I lay frozen in my bed. She was there to get me.

I was desperately searching for words to get rid of the being that had been with me for the past 18 years. The more I struggled with what to do, the more I realized who she was. It struck me like an icy snowball. She was evil, she was a demon. She was never good; she had withheld her true intentions and identity from me.

The room felt frozen, fear swirled around me. I knew I had to get rid of her. Something grabbed my throat, I couldn't speak and my mind turned to mush. Porgy continued to beckon me and I struggled to talk. After what seemed like 2 hours, but probably was only 2 minutes, it was as if something whispered; "say this." And with that suggestion, I was able to say six liberating words: "in the Name of Jesus, go." Immediately, the presence that followed me since I was 2 ½ years old exploded into grey flakes, tuned into grey smoke and dissipated right before my eyes. She was gone and I was free.

You see, unbeknownst to me during our relationship, her assignment was to make sure the gifts I was given were not used for God. By becoming aware of what was happening to me, I jeopardized her mission. The knowledge God was flooding into me threatened her stronghold over me. So she stepped up her game up and came for me. One final attempt for me to choose her and all she had meant to me over God.

As Porgy's presence dissipated, the scales on my eyes dissipated. I knew I had no business in that school. If I made it through the night, my life was going to change because I understood the distinction of which I was serving. I sat up the rest of the night, not knowing if something else was going to come for me. I could hear people walking around our complex and I could see flashlights and sirens. I was terrified and wanted to go home. Reality had sat in.

The next day I notified the school I would not be returning. I thanked God for delivering me from an unspeakable horror of a life. I packed my clothes and contacted my cousin who had been asking me to go to church with her while I was in California. I was always too busy; I had pulled further and further from God making my "high-jacking" a possibility. Not anymore. I went to my cousin and lived with her until I returned to Washington. My roommate thought I had lost my mind but she was conflicted because she knew *something* had happened to me, she didn't know what. I couldn't even explain the depth of understanding that exploded in me that night, and the deep and permanent discernment. God gave me these gifts and they were going to be used for His purpose only from that point on.

> *Joshua 24:14-16 (NIV)*
> *[14] "Now fear the Lord and serve him with all faithfulness. Throw away the gods your ancestors worshiped beyond the Euphrates River and in Egypt, and serve the Lord. [15] But if serving the Lord seems undesirable to you, then choose for yourselves this day whom you will serve, whether the gods your*

ancestors served beyond the Euphrates, or the gods of the Amorites, in whose land you are living. But as for me and my household, we will serve the Lord." ¹⁶ Then the people answered, "Far be it from us to forsake the Lord to serve other gods!

When I got home the first thing I did was gather all of my books, games and gadgets. I took them to the burning barrel in our backyard. With my sister by my side I put the items in, doused everything with lighter fluid and lit it. The flame shot high into the air. The smoke from the fire rose high and wide. It choked my sister and me. We moved to one side to get out of the way of the smoke; it followed. We moved in the other direction and the smoke followed. Anywhere we moved, the smoke followed. I got the water hose and put out the fire. That was the last time I had any involvement with the divination. I closed the chapter on those items and that subject as a naïve participant who got in way too deep. I do, however, have a permanent appreciation for what I have come to know as spiritual warfare and man's place of choice, between two spiritual forces.

How could I, a born again believer, have gotten myself so involved in the dark arts? Simple, I was ignorant about the Word of God. I had no one to teach me what I was doing was wrong. I was out of church more than I was in, and didn't allow my spiritual relationship with God to grow. I still looked to another source, other than my Creator and Sustainer, for answers. It was out of ignorance that a demon, a familiar spirit, a demonic angel was sent to watch over me and was able to stay with me for 18 years. Fortunately for me, Porgy was unable to finish its assignment because my angels intervened. I was brought to church to receive. John 14 and John 16 talk about God's Plan – the Father, Son and Holy Spirit working together to bring us to relationship with Him. When I made the decision eight years earlier to accept Jesus as my Lord and Savior, I belonged to God. He was fully prepared to protect me and guide me; I just had to acknowledge Him and let Him give me the answers to my deepest questions.

I didn't know at the time that God said he would never leave me or forsake me (Hebrews 13:5), but He kept his word. When we accept the gift of salvation (John 3:16) and become a "whosoever" unto God, we accept His love and with that comes protection of our purpose.

I'm so thankful that God assigned His angels who watched over me no matter how far I wandered. By doing what God originally created them to do. I was back on track and from those experiences; I was stronger and wiser for the journey.

FIVE

WALTER

Although my earlier years included far too much exposure to demons, my commitment to Christ, and the revelation God gave me that year at "college" resulted in a major life change. When I returned to college that spring, I began dating my husband to be, whom, unbeknownst to me, had a Pastoral calling.

We frequently prayed that God would put us in ministry together. Now for me I wasn't praying for Pastor and Wife ministry I was praying for regular couple of times a month ministry. At this point we had not discussed his calling and thank God for that. Had I known this then I would have ran like a gazelle. Why, because five years earlier I had an angelic visitation who told me things about my future life. The one piece of information that rocked me back on my heels was that I was going to marry a PASTOR so that would make me A PASTOR'S WIFE! That was the last thing I wanted to hear. My previous experiences with pastor's wives were not positive. I also had the innate awareness of the magnitude and responsibility that calling carried with it.

God does have a sense of humor or I should say He gets what he wants. We were married two years later. A week after our honeymoon we began a Bible study in our home. I was completely comfortable with the bible study. It was just a bible study right? I remember telling God one evening that it didn't look like the past prophesy from the angel was going to happen since my husband was not a Pastor. He was just a bible study teacher. I also thanked God for putting us in ministry together as we had prayed many times during our dating relationship. I thought I had it all worked out. Again unbeknownst to me my husband was very aware of his calling but knew it was not the time to tell me.

We had been married two years to the date when the next major event took place in my life. It was early one morning while we slept, I audibly heard "Terry get up". We both woke and sat up at the same time. I turned my head to see if my husband heard the same thing and noticed he was getting up and putting on his socks. I said to him, "did you hear that?" He said yes. I then said "sounds like he is serious" my husband said nothing but continued to get his socks on and left the room.

That night he told me he was called into the ministry and had to obey this time. He shared with me that he had received his calling seven months earlier but ignored it. This time the Lord said you go see your Pastor and you go now! I cried.

Five years later I finally came out of denial and accepted our calling. I knew if God gave me a peep into my future through the angelic vision and I innately knew what to do and what not to do as a Pastor's wife then he would provide whatever I needed to be the best Pastor's wife I could be. He has not let me down in our thirty-four years of ministry.
My next encounter with an Angel happened on Sunday, May 18, 1980. It was a beautiful Sunday morning. We had driven to Spokane Washington to watch my brother compete in a state track meet. We had a great time and he won.

We knew we had a six-hour drive ahead of us and wanted to get home before i dark so we awoke early the next morning, piled into our van and got on the road. We chatted about the track meet, what we were going to do when we got home, and where we were going to eat dinner. Music was playing, the sky was blue and it was a perfect day.

About an hour and a half into our drive, we noticed the sky ahead of us was dark. We watched for a few minutes hypothesizing about what could be causing the dark sky and rolling clouds. We realized the more we drove the closer the darkness came to us. We decided it was a dust storm. We all laughed; it would be just our luck to be caught in an Eastern Washington dust storm.

As we continued driving we noticed the dust storm was rolling towards us and growing larger. I'm thinking is that getting bigger because it's closer or is that...in the middle of my thoughts it began to rain down pellets. I remember saying that this was the biggest and hardest dust I had ever seen. The pelting of our van and an eerie grey black sky brought a deafening silence to our car. We slowed down because visibility was zero and we had to zig zag through the abandoned cars and trucks on the highway. I had never heard of a dust storm bringing the freeway to a halt. It felt like a movie set of a disaster film. Little did I know it was a disaster.

We were totally at a loss as to what was going on. Moving at a very slow pace we inched our way until we came upon flashing lights. Two state patrolmen wearing gas masks stopped us. We were startled not only because they seemed to appear out of nowhere but also the realization flooded our minds that there had to be a terrible problem. I felt like I had entered the twilight zone. At this point the pellets were hitting the windshield like a torrent rain. We rolled down the window and the officer said, "Where do you people think you are going?" We told him we were going to Seattle. He said, "Don't you people listen to the radio?" "Yes" we said. "We've had it on for the past 1 1/2 hours. He then said, "You can't get to Seattle, the mountain blew up!"

Have you ever seen those movies where the words that are spoken are so shocking that they echo, slow down and repeat several times in your head? Well that is what happened to me. It took about five seconds before we all said in shock; "WHAT!" Talk about feeling like someone punched you in the gut. We sat in silence until the officer said we would have to turn around and return to where we came from. We explained we had just come from Spokane for a track meet and didn't have anywhere else to go. He told us we couldn't head west and would have to turn around and head to the hospital in Moses Lakes where they were housing all of the travelers who were stranded."

So, we crossed over the median and headed back east towards Moses Lake. Questions hit our minds. Was everyone on the west side dead? What do we do next? Where do we go?

We took the first exit, which happened to be a truck stop. We knew we could get food, water and shelter. As we pulled into the truck stop it was obvious that we were not the only ones who were caught in the same predicament. The parking lot was full, no one was in sight and all of the motels had NO VACANCY signs. We parked in the Denny's parking lot. My husband and brother went to find temporary shelter and my sister-in-law and I headed in the direction of the Denny's. None of us had any idea what we looked like and what had happened to us while we were driving.

The door was locked and staring back at us was an over capacity crowd of people who would not open the door. They looked frightened and panicked. We tried to communicate through the locked door that we had to use the facilities but they wouldn't move. Finally a stressed out waitress opened the door with a stern warning. "Do what you need to do and be on your way, there is no room here". I could hear The Twilight Zone music playing in my head as we walked past the quiet group looking at us as if we were not human.

I was thinking what is wrong with them. I knew we were in Moses Lake but we looked like everyone else... I stopped in midstream of my internal conversation when after stepping into the restroom I understood the unusual stares. Staring back at us were our ghostly images, covered in ash from head to toe. That answered my question.

There were no hotel vacancies, we were in a strange town, in the dark at 11:30 in the afternoon, traumatized, unable to breathe or see very well and needed to get to the hospital. We left Denny's and I said Lord all we got is you and that is enough.

We headed back to the van and reached for the door when, a yellow VW spun around the corner, making doughnuts in the ash as if it was snow. My husband and brother came around the corner and told us that the kid in the car was willing to take us to the hospital. The kid jumped out of the car with a large smile and introduced himself as

Walter. We thanked him and praised God because we had just been saved from sleeping in the van. We hopped in the van, with Walter in the driver's seat, and off to the hospital we went.

The mood lightened as we headed to our destination. We were all talking about the mountain, what was happening on the west side when I noticed Walter was driving a little too fast for the conditions. I knew he knew where he was going but the ash was flying up and hitting the windshield causing visibility to be even more compromised. On top of that, Walter was using the windshield wipers on high speed, laughing, talking, turning his head and driving just as if it was a sunny day and he had an autopilot.

I was curious how he could drive so fast and see where he was going, but I was too thankful that he was willing to help us to bring it up. Instead, I said, "Walter, you came at the right time to help us, for all we know you might be an angel". He turned his head, looked at me, and with a smile and a wink said "you might be right". We all laughed, but I knew I had experienced something that was not from this earth. His eyes were the bluest of blues, like crystal diamonds. They pierced my spirit, soul and body. I couldn't, and to this day still can't, find the words to adequately describe them. I have seen those eyes on other "beings" and I know, and they know I know, that they are full of God's grace and compassion. I have talked to people who have encountered angels before as well and the first thing they talk about is the color of their eyes.

A little prick of excitement hit my body as it registered that Walter was not just an ordinary man. I sat back and didn't worry about the speed because I knew God was in control and I was excited to see what was going to happen.

We arrived at the hospital in about five minutes. It was packed. People were everywhere. The staff were people just like us with their own families and concerns and yet they were nice and accommodating but clearly dealing with a true crisis. We checked in, got our eyes flushed and received breathing treatments. We were clean, fed and happy. We wandered the hospital talking to people from all over the United States. It's amazing how people come together when there is a crisis.

We tried calling our families but couldn't get through. There was nothing we could do except stay put; we had to trust that God had taken care of our families on the west side of the mountain just as He was taking care of us on the eastside. The hours passed as we talked, played games, walked through the hospital and discussed how we were going to get home.

On one of my trips around the hospital, I wandered into the physician's lounge. The door to a locker was open and on the inside of the door was a map of the city. Moses Lake was bigger than I thought. I got curious and wanted to locate the hospital on the map. I found the truck stop and traced...traced...wow that was a long way. It looked to me like the distance between the truck stop and the hospital would have taken more than a few minutes. I stopped one of the nurses coming into the lounge and asked her how long it would take for someone to drive that distance. She said on a good day about 15 minutes. I asked, "What about now?" referring to the impossible conditions the volcanic eruption had created. She laughed, "You would not have made it. The roads are all impassable and the major road leading to the hospital is closed." Time, again, stood still for me. I knew in that moment that my inkling about Walter was accurate. Walter truly was an angel sent from the Almighty God.

I went looking for my family to share what I had just discovered. Walter and the guys were having a ball - laughing, joking and teasing each other. It was like they were old friends who reconnected. I walked up just as the fellas were headed for the restroom. I kept watching Walter to see if he would give us another indication that he was an angel but he acted like one of the boys. I told my sister-in-law about the map. She laughed and said I'm not surprised at anything today. A few minutes later, the fellas came busting out of the restroom holding their noses. Apparently there was a very offensive odor that had them coming apart at the seams. Walter was right in the middle of the fun.

About 5:00 pm that evening there was an announcement that we were being transported to local homes for the night. We would be staying there until we were able to leave. I was so happy because I knew that meant a bed. We gathered our belongings and prepared for our transport.

Over the loud speaker we heard that our bus was loading, but I had to get my curiosity satisfied before we left. I asked Walter how he was going to get home since he had left his car in the parking lot. He told me his father lived a few blocks from the hospital so he could walk to his home. I asked him if he was sure he would be ok? With that, Walter smiled and with a glint in those crystal blue eyes he said, "I'm going to my Father's house and I'll be fine". We all paused and stood in the corridor for a few moments in silence. It wasn't what he said but the way he said it. I said, "Can we get your father's phone number so we can call and make sure you are safe?" He gave us a number with a bunch of seven's in it. We collected our belongings and went to walk with Walter and say our last goodbyes when we noticed Walter was no longer standing with us. We turned our heads to the left and could see him rounding the corner heading out of the hospital. We yelled for Walter to wait, he looked back and waved at us with that big smile on his face. We ran down the corridor and out the front door but we could not see Walter. We ran to the end of the street, no Walter. We doubled back, no Walter. We walked back into the hospital dumbfounded. No one could have moved that fast...and it hit all of us at the same time...Walter was an angel. I said, "I bet there won't be an answer to that phone number when we call it," and there wasn't.

We talked about Walter walking to the bus. We shared stories with each other and all of them were different. We also had different descriptions of him. You see Walter had brought books with him when he got into the van. His intention was to drop us off and continue on to his journey (or so he said). Interestingly, as we compared notes, each of us saw different books and heard a different story from Walter. My husband saw concordances and study Bibles; Walter told him that he was heading to his dad's house to do a little biblical research on a project they were working on. He was a tall lean kid with brown hair. My brother saw music books; Walter told him he was letting a friend borrow them. My sister-in-law saw a couple of reading books with folders. Walter, having told her that he was going to go home and read the afternoon away. I saw science and quantum physics books and he had told me he was heading to his girlfriend's house to study for a test. He was average height with blonde hair. One thing we all agreed on was that he did not have any ash on him or his car. It and he were completely clean even though he was in the same situation we were in.

What a humbling day. We were so thankful for God's loving kindness and divine protection. Who were we that He would look down on us and provide such a wonderful experience? We were dropped off at our host home and had a wonderful dinner. Our host family were vegetarians, "so where's the meat" jokes went on all night. It was so much fun. We were still basking in the Walter experience.

The next day we found out everyone west of the mountain was fine and there was a window of opportunity to leave. We quickly got in our van and headed to the rendezvous spot. There was a long line of ashy vehicles waiting and ready to make the caravan trip through the northern tip of the state. In the daylight, we could see the devastation the mountain had caused. It only confirmed to us the blessing we had experienced. Before we pulled out of Moses Lake, I called the number again. No answer.

We made it to the exit site. There was a state patrolman counting the cars as they got in line. The line stretched in front and behind us as far as the eye could see. The state patrol placed a sign that read, "Last car in line. Try tomorrow" behind our van. We were the last to leave that day. We found out later that all the cars behind us were stranded on the east side of the mountain for six days before they reopened the pass again. God was good to us. I don't think the fellas could have lasted six days without meat.

Once again, God blessed and He did it through supernatural intervention

Family and friends awaited our return. They knew about the devastation caused by the eruption and had not talked to us until that morning. It was a joyous and thankful reunion. We were also thankful that we made the long seven-hour trip because the van was an antique and caused us concern even in the best conditions.

We were so happy to be with our family and friends; we spent the rest of the day and evening sharing our miraculous angel story.

The next day my brother took his van into the shop to be flushed and inspected. The ash caused irreparable damage to all forms of transportation. There were countless stories of engines being completely ruined because of the ash.

After inspecting the engine the mechanic asked my brother why he brought his van in and what was he suppose to be looking for. He told the mechanic he wanted his engine flushed because we had been in Eastern Washington and he was concerned about the ash in his engine. The mechanic asked, "you were over there when the mountain blew?" My brother answered yes. The mechanic said, "There is no way you were over there, stop joking with me". My brother assured him that we were there. The mechanic informed my brother that people who had been over there IF they made it back had to replace their engines and pay for major damages to their cars. He told my brother that he didn't have <u>any</u> ash in his engine or inside of the car. They argued back and forth until my brother realized God had protected his van. Can you believe that, the creator and sustainer of life protecting a van?

Walking around the van and thanking God my brother noticed a small pool of ash sitting on the inside of the front bumper. He called the mechanic over to see the proof. The mechanic was speechless and my brother continued to thank God for having his angels watch over all of us, in big and small ways.

SIX

THE FIRE

I t was an early Monday morning after the end of our six-show run of our church production called "The Open Door." We had guest in our home for the week and my husband had gotten up early to take our company to the airport.

After he left, I couldn't sleep so I got up and started my day. I was combing my hair in the bathroom when I heard a faint clanging. I ignored it because it sounded like it was coming from outside and the city was always working on something in our neighborhood.

A few minutes later the clanging got louder. I thought they must be right in front of my house because it was so loud. What could they be doing so early in the morning? A few moments later, a banging joined the clanging, which was met with the fire alarm. I knew then something was happening inside of my house. I ran out of the bathroom and as I rounded the corner heading into the living room, I could smell smoke. The sound and smell were overwhelming as flames shot out of the wall.

I was stunned for a moment and thought I was having a nightmare. It became all too real when the flames began to climb the steps to the second floor. The second floor was where our three-year-old son was asleep in his bedroom.
Time was ticking as I tried to figure out how to put out the flames. The fire was too large to throw a pan of water on it

so I stood there in limbo. Then horror hit me as I watched the staircase catch fire and heard my three-year-old son's scream. The fire alarm woke him up and the smoke was choking him. I had to get to him

Without thinking and in a tricot nightgown, I bolted up the flaming stairs, grabbed my son, and ran down the stairs thru the flames and to the back door where I called 911. By now the entire entryway, lower half of the stairs and living room curtains were engulfed in flames.

I gave my address to the fire department and hung up the phone. Within minutes I could hear the sirens. I examined my son. He was scared, but fine. My clothing was singed, but I was also fine. We both were chocking.

I looked towards the fire to assess the damage and realized the front door was shut and I wouldn't be able to open it unless I went back through the fire. How were the firemen going to get in? I decided I would go out the back door and flag them down. As I recalculated my options, my world went into slow motion and I turned towards the front door just in time to see a man walk up the walkway carrying a fire extinguisher, enter my house, smiled at me, and put out the flames. He never said a word; turned to leave, looked back at me, smiled and walked out the door. He came just in time to handle the flames before it became a complete disaster.

As he disappeared around the corner, my world went back to normal speed. At that moment I saw my neighbor appear at my door. I told her to catch the gentleman that just walked past her. She gave me this confused look like she didn't understand me. I again this time in a raised voice told her to go get the man that just passed her. She slowly shook her head and said, "no one passed me." I told her she just passed the man who put the fire out. I asked her to hurry and go get him because I wanted to thank him. She insisted that no one passed her and said I must have been hallucinating because of the smoke inhalation. The house was full of smoke and the clanging from the wall heater was still making its deafening sound. My mind went into spiritual slow motion again for a few seconds as I replayed what I saw. I came back to reality with my friend shouting my name, fire trucks arriving and her looking at me as if I had lost my mind.

Several firemen and their equipment entered my house. Even though the fire was out in the stairwell and living room, it was still in the walls. They went to work tearing my wall apart while the medics examined my son and me. The fire chief told me that I had done a good job putting the fire out. He said I prevented a major catastrophe because I lived in a town house complex and the entire street could have gone up in flames because of the type of fire and the location in which it started. I wanted to tell him that I didn't do anything but I realized they would have looked at me just like my neighbor did.

I silently thanked God for His goodness mercy and grace. He had me get up when my husband left so that I would be awake when the fire started. He gave me extraordinary stamina to run through flaming steps to grab my baby and jump over four steps that were on fire. I was not hurt. Everything was done "just in the nick of time" because there was no additional seconds to spare.

God sent his angel to put the fire out that day and I often

think about that morning. One thing still puzzles me. My front door was closed and locked when I ran down the steps with my son. I never opened the door because the entryway was on fire and my only purpose was to get my son and me away from the fire. That same door, which was closed, was opened when my heavenly firefighter entered and saved our home. That door was also open when the "real" firefighters arrived. There was plenty of evidence that an extinguisher had been discharged – just not by me or any human.

Now here is the big blessing. We had just gotten renters insurance the week before and they paid for the entire remodel. God was good to us. We were physically and financially preserved from a heater malfunction that is rarely detected and often fatal.

I'm so grateful that my angel was watching over my son and me.

SEVEN

THE ACCIDENT

The morning began strangely. It was grey and raining, but that's not the strange part when you live in the Pacific Northwest. It felt like something had shifted spiritually but I couldn't put my finger on what was wrong. It seemed like something big was going to happen and that it wasn't good, which didn't make a lot of sense given we were ready to travel to Oregon to visit our son in college.

The heaviness continued that morning while we prepared for the trip. The SUV was filled with a care package for our son and our necessities. The most important thing in the car was the 36-inch television, not a flat screen. We had our son's car. He was disappointed he could not take the car and TV with him when he originally left. So we thought letting him have his TV and drive his car for the weekend would be a great treat. As we finished loading the car, the heaviness swirled around me like a buzzing black cloud. It was disconcerting. We started our trip; praying and trusting God that He would protect us.

Riding in a car for long distances was not my most favorite thing to do so I kept my mind preoccupied with conversation, reading and listening to music. My husband, nicknamed "Mario Andretti," was in the fast lane trying to do the speed limit. By all appearances we were making good time, the weather was breaking and it was quiet. But no matter how many nice thoughts, conversations or songs I had or listened to, I continued to have those brooding feelings and so I prayed.

I was looking at a field of cows when a white Ford Explorer passed us so fast it made us look like we were standing still. I remarked to my husband that if the driver wasn't careful he could end up rolling his SUV. We then talked about the rollovers that had happened with SUV's and how the roofs caved in. That probably wasn't a good conversation to have because we were driving an SUV. But we felt safe in ours because we knew God would protect us.

As the time went by, the feeling of dread became more intense. My prayers increased. I felt a dark shadow hanging over the top of the car. It felt like there was an intense battle happening right over our heads as we drove. As my feelings of intensity increased I had a strange need to lower my seat and put a pillow on the window and lay my head on it. I thought maybe I was tired and needed some rest. After all I didn't sleep well the night before because I was excited and thought maybe these "feelings" were just my excitement turned into anxiety. While I was preparing to lie down, my husband decided to reduce his speed and move into the slow lane.

As soon as we got into the slow lane we heard a loud bang as if someone had shot a gun. The car shook violently, swerved to the right, flipped, and rolled over three times (according to witnesses) down the freeway. We came to a dead stop in a ravine. As reality unfolded before us, I could hear my husband asking me if I was okay. I heard the engine racing, dust settling and tires screeching.

In a flash people rushed to our SUV and pried the doors

The impact had crushed them. As they took us from the vehicle, I could see my husband bleeding profusely from his upper arm; and could hear people shouting for a tourniquet. I on the other hand, couldn't talk and felt extremely light headed.

Time was immeasurable. I heard many voices, saw many faces but couldn't put it all together. I remember hearing a man say "that was awesome, that Durango flipped three times." Someone told him to shut up.

A woman, who was a nurse, put a tourniquet on my husband's arm and the next thing I knew there were two medics trying to coax me onto a backboard. I remember saying, "I'm a big girl. Can you handle me?" The medics laughed and told me they were big men and I would be fine. Once I saw them, they were right.

The trip to the hospital was a combination of sirens, medics talking, beeping noises, flashes of flipping over, angel wings and unusual sounds, which ran through my mind and in front of my eyes. I heard the medics talking to the ER doctor relaying my injuries. They said I was unresponsive, I kept yelling in my head "No, I'm not!" but the words wouldn't come out. They said my blood pressure was very high, that I had multiple contusions and that I was tachycardic. I was screaming in my head, "I can hear you!" Then my vanity kicked in and I told myself, "Girl, you better get stable before they rip or cut something." So I prayed, "Lord, please get me stable" and sure enough a warm comforting hand swept over me, like a blanket with a hug. I began breathing normally and made a few noises. The medics noticed I was responding and started talking to me again. I could barely get answers out but it was enough. I heard them downgrade my status. I thought, "Thank you, Jesus." I knew then that whatever came next, He'd face it with me.

Arriving at the hospital, I was rushed into the Emergency Room. Then the unthinkable happened, they ripped my shirt and pants. My favorite black pants with a small thin white stripe. It's funny what the mind thinks about when you are in shock. I must have looked a mess because the doctor asked if I was my husband's mother. The entire staff gasped at the same time. One of them said, "Are you kidding me? There is no way she can be his mother!" I laughed and said "no." Then a sobering thought hit me, I hope he was not going to be the one in charge of me! I didn't have much confidence in his skill level from that point on.

I still didn't feel as bad as the chatter between the medical staff indicated and couldn't understand what all the fuss was about until I was wheeled into the x-ray department. The x-ray technician lifted my arm to take a picture, and I screamed. The pain shot up my underarm and down to my waist. Looking at my upper arm I had a large grapefruit size contusion that "hung" about two inches below my arm. They checked me from head to toe and found multiple bruises, along with a fractured right elbow and a torn rotator cuff. They also found that I had suffered a serious concussion.

After several hours of testing and my vitals stabilized, they decided to release me. As I was wheeled out of the dark room and into the light I had a violent reaction. My head started spinning, I got nauseated and started heaving, my ears rang and the headache was unbearable. They took me back into the room. After three more failed attempts a nurse said, "I'm thinking we need to admit her". Wisdom was spoken. And where was my husband? Trying to get back to our car and drive my son's things to college. He was also in shock.

In the hospital that night I heard the nurses talking about the business of the day. One nurse said, "Yeah, can you believe two rollovers in one day when does that happen?" They got into a discussion about the dangers of Sports Utility Vehicles. Then what they said next perked my natural and spiritual ears up. They talked about the other people in the SUV that rolled before ours. I thought to myself could that have been the one that went barreling past us? The other nurse asked, "Is the Explorer survivor in #34? The other said, "No, the Explorer couple didn't make it. She and her husband were in the Durango. The husband was released and the wife is in #34. I don't know how they survived."

I later learned that the police and tow truck driver were amazed that we survived. The roof, front end and doors of the Durango were crushed but we weren't crushed. My husband a 6' 2" man survived the crushing of a SUV roof. His head was not on a pillow and he was not in a reclining position. I laid in my bed, head throbbing, arm in a cast, aching all over and Praised my Jesus for saving us. Right before I drifted off to sleep, I thanked God for our safety because I knew our angels watched over us that day. The unction to pray along with the prayers of our family and friends for our safety kept us alive and of course I have to give thanks to our Angels.

Amazingly, the TV, computer, lamps (items we were taking to my son) and even my sunglasses were all perfectly fine. Nothing was broken that was being transported; it was as if something held everything in place as we rolled down the highway.

My husband has his own story about the conversation he had with God during the roll over. It is the experiences like this that we know for sure that we are in a battle. When you are a threat to the enemy, you become a target. Evil marks you, and as I showed you in earlier chapters, knows when and where you might be most vulnerable, but God also moves in us and for us to counter those attacks. Prayers go up, angels move, and angels intervene so that we can continue to do the work God has appointed for us to do.

> *Isaiah 54:17 (KJV)*
> [17] *No weapon that is formed against thee shall prosper; and every tongue that shall rise against thee in judgment thou shalt condemn. This is the heritage of the servants of the Lord, and their righteousness is of me, saith the Lord.*

> *Luke 10:19 (KJV)*
> [19] *Behold, I give unto you power to tread on serpents and scorpions, and over all the power of the enemy: and nothing shall by any means hurt you.*

EIGHT

ENCOURAGEMENT

Once Porgy left and I began my intended journey with God, Angels become very important to me especially in ministry. Here are a just a few stories about how our angels watched and continue to watch over us.

Motorcycle Man

I remember one time early in ministry we were very discouraged. We prayed and sought the Lord for answers, a word of encouragement, anything to stabilize us; we needed to hear from our Father that night.

We were sitting on the front bumper of our car talking about how God had taken care of us up to date and we believed He would continue to do so, when we heard the roar of a motorcycle to our left. The more we talked, the louder the motorcycle roared until we couldn't ignore it anymore. As we turned our heads to see who was on the cycle, time went into slow motion. What I have heard over and over again as well as experienced is that sometimes when you are visited by Heavenly beings it is as if time shifts into slow motion feeling like a dream.

The rider drove right up to us, took his helmet off, looked us both in the eyes and patted us on our knees. Time shifted back to normal as he drove off. We jumped off the car and ran to catch him, but to no avail. When we rounded the corner, there was no motorcycle, no man, nothing. It was as if he disappeared.

We looked at each other and knew we had just been in the company of an angel. God heard our cry and he answered by sending a motorcycle riding black man with those crystal blue eyes that we both saw and experienced simultaneously. What was even more profound was the message of peace, calmness and the assurance that He was still in control and was handling our concerns. The message was given to us in "a blink of an eye." It was an amazing experience. I can still feel and see that event as if it happened yesterday. It was another blessing of an angel watching over us. This one sent to minister God's love and care for us.

God's presence is one of encouragement and hope. Whether you see the angel, or just benefit from the spirit's presence, you are made instantly better in ways that words cannot express.

2 Corinthians 1:2-4 (KJV)
2 Grace be to you and peace from God our Father, and from the Lord Jesus Christ. 3 Blessed be God, even the Father of our Lord Jesus Christ, the Father of mercies, and the God of all comfort; 4 Who comforteth us in all our tribulation, that we may be able to comfort them which are in any trouble, by the comfort wherewith we ourselves are comforted of God.

Isaiah 61:1 (KJV)
61 The Spirit of the Lord God is upon me; because the Lord hath anointed me to preach good tidings unto

the meek; he hath sent me to bind up the brokenhearted, to proclaim liberty to the captives, and the opening of the prison to them that are bound;

DESPONDENT

After three miscarriages I was at my end. I struggled with depression, I was miserable and I had lost hope. The doctors told me that I would never be able to have children. I knew what God could do, but it was taking all I had to stand on my wobbly faith and hold onto the promise that I would become a mother.

Early one morning, I woke up with a heavy heart. I felt like I had no place to turn. I went into another room to pray and ask God to please help me. I was so despondent that I didn't even have words to say to God. All I said was, "Lord Help me. I'm so sad". I cried and cried and cried.

At the height of my despair, the room shifted and time went into slow motion. Two large figures filled the room and the peace that surpasses all understanding (Philippians 4:7) settled within me. What I needed the most at that moment was a comforting touch and that is just what he provided. Yes I said he because I knew the beings were male. I didn't see anything but their torsos but I knew.

The larger one bent down and wrapped his arms around me. It felt like he lifted me off of the ground and encircled me in a warm embrace. It was healing. He gently released me and my sorrow, despair and fear all left.

The room went back to normal and I sat on the floor in total peace. I got up, went back to bed and once again knew that not only God, in general, but also specific angels had been assigned to watch over me. They are always there, but have consistently revealed themselves at the most vulnerable moments in my life.

THE MIRACLE

As you could imagine, when our son was born, after 2 miscarriages, and one tubal pregnancy, I was a bit neurotic about his safety. At the time I didn't think I was neurotic but I was. I was so worried that something was going to happen to him I would check on him relentlessly to the point that I couldn't get any rest. Finally my husband told me I had to trust God to take care of our son. Since God performed a miracle to bring him into this world, God could definitely take care of him. So I prayed for God to protect him and calm my nerves.

We noticed that when our son was in his crib, he would be singing and gurgling or cooing. It was as if he was playing with someone. At first we thought that it was a cute anomaly, but then we noticed there was a pattern to his noises. So one day we quietly went into his room and as we entered we saw the torso of an angel as it was leaving. I guess he didn't like us interrupting his conversation with our son. When he left, our son got frustrated and was fussy as if we took something from him. From that point on when we heard our son cooing and laughing in his crib, we would just smile. We knew that either he was entertaining the angel, or the angel was entertaining him. Either way, they had a connection and God had given us a glimpse of the intervention it took to bring our son into this world, and the protection God intended for him while he grew up.

Too this day I don't worry about him and his family. I know God takes care of them and we got to witness the angel assigned to him from his very beginnings.

You should never doubt that angels are watching over you. It is their assignment from God. You might not feel like it, you might wonder about it, but I encourage you to explore it. Start with an understanding of who you are serving, and what influences you are allowing to enter into your life. If you begin this journey by thinking of God in terms of a relationship, and you being the prize, you may be able to see the work of angels in your own life.

> 1 John 4:1-5 (NIV)
> [1] Dear friends, do not believe every spirit, but test the spirits to see whether they are from God, because many false prophets have gone out into the world. [2] This is how you can recognize the Spirit of God: Every spirit that acknowledges that Jesus Christ has come in the flesh is from God, [3] but every spirit that does not acknowledge Jesus is not from God. This is the spirit of the antichrist, which you have heard is coming and even now is already in the world. [4] You, dear children, are from God and have overcome them, because the one who is in you is greater than the one who is in the world. [5] They are from the world and therefore speak from the viewpoint of the world, and the world listens to them

God says that we shouldn't be ignorant about spiritual things. The ability to "distinguish between spirits" also called spiritual discernment is an important gift from God. It is a gift that some might have a greater aptitude for, but each of us has the chance to develop out of a growing relationship with God.

1 Corinthians 12: 1-11 (NIV)
Concerning Spiritual Gifts
1 Now about the gifts of the Spirit, brothers and sisters, I do not want you to be uninformed. 2 You know that when you were pagans, somehow or other you were influenced and led astray to mute idols. 3 Therefore I want you to know that no one who is speaking by the Spirit of God says, "Jesus be cursed," and no one can say, "Jesus is Lord," except by the Holy Spirit. 4 There are different kinds of gifts, but the same Spirit distributes them. 5 There are different kinds of service, but the same Lord. 6 There are different kinds of working, but in all of them and in everyone it is the same God at work. 7 Now to each one the manifestation of the Spirit is given for the common good. 8 To one there is given through the Spirit a message of wisdom, to another a message of knowledge by means of the same Spirit, 9 to another faith by the same Spirit, to another gifts of healing by that one Spirit, 10 to another miraculous powers, to another prophecy, to another distinguishing between spirits, to another speaking in different kinds of tongues, and to still another the interpretation of tongues. 11 All these are the work of one and the same Spirit, and he distributes them to each one, just as he determines.

With both angels and demons watching over us, we have a responsibility to become wiser about the life we are called to live.

Epilogue

Jesus tell us in 1 Corinthians 13:12 that;

> 12 *In the same way, we can see and understand only a little about God now, as if we were peering at his reflection in a poor mirror; but someday we are going to see him in his completeness, face-to-face. Now all that I know is hazy and blurred, but then I will see everything clearly, just as clearly as God sees into my heart right now.*

I look forward to going home and seeing "everything clearly." I look forward to meeting my angels who took care of me all of my human life, what a reunion that will be!

As I said in the beginning of the book, I shared these stories so that it may inspire you to move closer to God. The closer you get to Him the more your spiritual eyes will open. Once you see **them** you to one day might have your own angels' stories to write about.

ABOUT THE AUTHOR

GiGi Rogers lives in the Pacific Northwest with her husband. She loves writing, sewing, spending time with friends and most of all being grandma.

For more information contact GiGi at;
GiGI_Rogers@aol.com

www.ingramcontent.com/pod-product-compliance
Lightning Source LLC
Chambersburg PA
CBHW071905020426
42331CB00010B/2673